The Planet on the Desk

Other poetry books by David Young

Sweating Out the Winter
(University of Pittsburgh Press, 1969)

Boxcars
(Ecco Press, 1973)

Work Lights: Thirty-two Prose Poems
(Cleveland State University Poetry Center, 1977)

The Names of a Hare in English
(University of Pittsburgh Press, 1979)

Foraging
(Wesleyan University Press, 1986)

Earthshine
(Wesleyan University Press, 1988)

Wesleyan University Press

Published by
University Press of New England
Hanover and London

David Young

The
Planet
on the
Desk

Selected and New Poems   1960–1990

Wesleyan University Press
Published by University Press of New England, Hanover, NH 03755

Printed in the United States of America   5 4 3 2 1

CIP data appear at the end of the book

Some of the poems in "New Poems" previously appeared in *The Antioch Review, Fine Madness,* and *New England Quarterly.*

Contents

I: from *Sweating Out the Winter* (1969)

The Man Who Swallowed a Bird   3
Putting It Mildly   4
Late Summer: Lake Erie   5
Poem about Hopping   6
Segal   7
More about Skills   8
Sweating Out the Winter   9
Nineteen Sixty-three   11
Two Renewal Poems   12

II: from *Boxcars* (1973)

The Boxcar Poem   15
Three for the Moon   16
Homing   18
In Heaven   22
Mandelstam   23
Thoughts of Chairman Mao   26
Ohio   29
Love Song   31
Chromos   32
Notes on the Poems   35
A Calendar: The Beautiful Names of the Months   37
Teddy Roosevelt   39
Woodrow Wilson   40
from Water Diary   41

III: from *Work Lights: Thirty-Two Prose Poems* (1977)

The Poem against the Horizon   47
Four about the Letter P   48
Four about Heavy Machinery   50
Four about Death   52
Four about Mummies   54
Kohoutek   56

IV: from *The Names of a Hare in English* (1979)

Two Views of the Cathedral   59
Nineteen Forty-four   60
"Other Forms Were Near": Five Words   62
How Music Began   64
Three Time-Trips   65
The Day Nabokov Died   67
The Picture Says   69
Jaywalker   70
Tool Talk   71
After My Death   72
A Lowercase Alphabet   73
from The Names of a Hare in English
   Les Nouns de un levre en Engleis   75
   Just an old poem. Beyond us   77
   In the time before dawn, in graylight   77
   Along the Vermilion River   79
   We have some quiet families in this neighborhood   80
   Shakespeare's portrait hangs in my office   80
   I look at the backs of my hands and get lost   81
   A day swings past. A husk of hares   82

V: from *Foraging* (1986)

In My Own Back Yard   85
A Ghost, to One Alive   88
Two Trips to Ireland   89
October Couplets   92
Basho   95
The Self: A Sonnet Sequence   99
Hunting for Mushrooms in Orange County   105
Suite for Jean Follain   106
Elegy in the Form of an Invitation   108
Vermont Summer: Three Snapshots, One Letter   110
Three Walks   113

VI: from *Earthshine* (1988)

The Moon-Globe   117
from Nine Deaths   118
   Surgery   118
   Seizure   118
   Anemia   120
   Heart Failure   121
   Coda   122
From Poem in Three Parts   124
   from Broken Field Running   124
      What stands on one leg at night?   124
      And isn't the earth our goddess?   124
      Nineteen-oh-five   126
      My garret in New Haven   126

from Dancing in the Dark   127
    October three. Jade-green, Plum Creek slides by   127
    "Rabbits in Alabama hop," I wrote in 1963   128
    Industrial sky this afternoon, gray rags   128
    A London Saturday. One year ago   130
    I'm watching the brown tangle of tomato vines   131
from The Light Show   132
    Today the April light is fizzing   132
    Gaze of Apollo, that kindled Rilke   133
    Light in the mountains — the Andes, in this case —   133
    Earthrise: from its rubbled moon   134
    It's a late October afternoon   136
The Portable Earth-Lamp   137

VII: New Poems

Visionary's Ghazal   141
Root Vegetable Ghazal   142
Adolescence Ghazal   143
Easter Ghazal   144
Autumn Ghazal   145
Bird Ghazal   146
Hamlet Ghazal   147
Stevens Ghazal   148
Worship Ghazal   149
Mirror Ghazal   150

I

from

Sweating
Out
the Winter

1969

The Man Who Swallowed a Bird

Happened when he was yawning.
A black or scarlet bird went down his throat
And disappeared, and at the time
He only looked foolish, belched a feather;
The change took time.

But when we saw him again in the
Half-dusk of a summer evening
He was a different man. His eyes
Glittered and his brown hands
Lived in the air like swallows;
Knowledge of season lit his face
But he seemed restless. What he said
Almost made sense, but from a distance:

> Once I swallowed a bird,
> Felt like a cage at first, but now
> Sometimes my flesh flutters and I think
> I could go mad for joy.

In the fall he vanished. South
Some said, others said dead. Jokes
About metamorphosis were made. Nonetheless,
Some of us hear odd songs.

                        Suppose
You press your ear against the morning air,
Above and on your left you might
Hear music that implies without a word
A world where a man can absorb a bird.

Putting It Mildly

Into the uproar of April emerged Mr. Marblearch,
Ready again to be well aware of the weather,
For a normal informal part in the burgeoning season's
Annual matters of magnitude.

Like a cat encountering cream he encountered the colors
And tapped his cigar so as not to endanger the flowers;
He paused in thought by a solemn and wild forsythia,
Fancies assailing his head.

"This sun," Mr. Marblearch said, "is enlarged
Like the oldest idea enjoying its newest form
In an epochal fashion. Ahem. It is like a sublime
Balloon that will never burst.

"Furthermore," he went on, beneath a magnolia,
"To have a sky in one's head, a bush in the breast,
Is to partake of the pattern, the bee and the tree
Being in season."

Marblearch colored in the season's din
With the whole magnolia, alive on the grass
In the role of forsythia, feeling the morning sun's
Ideas hot on his face.

In memory of Wallace Stevens

Late Summer: Lake Erie

Nearly a year since word of death
Broke off the summer: as if a goddess
You followed respectfully
Should turn and stun you with her look.

We can go back to Old Woman Creek,
Easy canoeing except where lotus
And water lily choke the way:
Rose mallows massed on the banks, around
Bends, the sudden rise of ducks,
Invisible bitterns, the silent, ponderous
Heron, our kingfisher escort,
And, under the still, flowering
Surface, death: the orange carp
Crowd toward the killer lake.

I swore I'd write no letters to the dead.
It's only myself I want to tell
Things are about the same. The wind
Still pounds and stumbles around the cottage,
The lake is streaked and rumpled, dead
Fish wash up to the beach, our summer
Is the same, sweet, easily murdered pleasure.
I wade in the supple breakers, I'll
Paddle again on the creek. Now,
This morning, I walk to the road;
All to the south the dazed, hot landscape lies,
Under its piled thunderheads,
Dreaming of love and survival.

Poem about Hopping

Rabbits in Alabama hop
Into clumps of Syrian grass
To nibble the stalks, thinking of
Sorghum, hardly noticing autumn.

Along the Great Divide the bighorn
Sheep hop casually from rock to
Rock in the wind and glare, seriously
Considering leaping silver rivers, as

Salmon in crazy waters jump
Upstream for love—oh, it's
A nervous country. When you
Walk through stubble, the hub

Of a wheel with grasshopper
Spokes, or sit over bowls of excited
Cereal, what can you say to your heart
But, Down sir, down sir, down?

Segal

The girl who sits on the bed
Facing the window while her lover sleeps

Leans, hands on the mattress, into
A blue, enormously late, light,

Her arms, face, breasts all turning
Blue while she thinks about nothing

But simply carries her sorrow
And is unconscious of her beauty

While in the room where the sculptor
Has put her, the light comes slowly

Back to bright, as her white skin
Grows whiter, her flesh more solid,

She, her lover, the bed, unstained
By color or darkness, polar, thick,

As if the light could take us unaware
When we knew least that we were what

We hoped we'd be, calm and intact;
As if the light could give us what we lacked.

More about Skills

I saw myself talking
At a distance, hands busy

With the air: scooping it,
Shaping it, drawing it out,

And brushing it away,
A story of hands and arms.

The words were lost like smoke
But the gestures were ancient

Signs that I took to say:
How do we know our medium

Except we divide it
With our hands, breaking its bread,

Pouring its thin wine. Here
Is a batch I have gathered,

Before it disperses, inspect
It, sift and caress it,

Carry it weightless on your
Wrists, your unmapped palms,

Drink it, spring in the blood,
Return it in smoky words,

Words that beget gestures,
Gestures assembling the air.

Sweating Out the Winter

Like an old pot on the stove
My head simmers and rattles.
Outside, beyond the window,
A cloud of steam from the dryer
Rises through steadily falling snow.

In the warm sack of my body
I drowse, losing the past.

The land remembers its huge snows,
The death of animals
(Hay bales dropped
For the stiffening cattle).

The water, its skin turned
Brittle as bird bones by the wind,
Remembers summer like a soft,
Blowing steam.

My palms are wet. Blinking,
I lean toward the window.

Forests and wastes.
Blank white lakes.

In the distance a city
Steams and smokes on the cold plain
Under gray and ivory clouds.
I close my eyes. More wastes!
Massed ice, the flecked dome
Of father Eisenhower! The soft
Groans of freezing hoboes (bodies
That won't be found until the thaw),
Speeches for reform, crowds,
Cries and thuds at the line of scrimmage.

And quiet. The noiseless
Snowing, small women asleep
In white-and-gilt bedrooms,
The president's coffin, centered
In the rotunda, below the dome,
The Texaco station on the corner
Where laid-off workers loiter.

Come north, hums the wind
Off the ice cap. In vast white wastes
The caribou survive.
To know how to store
Warmth! In his skin boat
The Eskimo sets out, a precarious
Floating. I reach out.
The pane clouds at my touch and then
Begins to clear.

Nineteen Sixty-three

The year the president was killed
Was the same my friend was shot
On a Washington street one night
For his white skin and wallet.

What we can't bear we bury.
I got so I thought I could
Stand the abruptness if only
There were some final word.

But when he returned in a dream
Dying and bleached like Gracchus,
And there was a chance to explain,
We were both shy and speechless.

Then I grew light with wonder
Watching beside the bed,
My stubbornness fell away
For I thought I understood

That he wouldn't elect to live
Here at the end of the myth
If he could, and I smiled and said,
"You're the President of Death."

Two Renewal Poems

1 The Line

What weather is this?
My body is heavy, real; it walks
Out of the house, into the wind.
My small son watches from the window;
I wave and walk away.
A blue jay stalls
Above a spruce. My
Forehead touches the cold glass.
My father waves
And walks away.

2 The Circle

Driving across Iowa
In the corn-green light, you
Sometimes come across
Between the road and pasture
A knee-high gush of water
From a deep artesian well
Rising and tumbling into itself
In the raw sun, cold and sweet.

You stand at the center of summer,
Your life rising and falling.

Take a tin can from the fence post.
Drink.

II

from

Boxcars

1973

The Boxcar Poem

The boxcars drift by
clanking

they have their own
speech on scored
wood sheet
metal their own
calligraphy
Soo Line
they say in meadows
Lackawanna quick at crossings
Northern Pacific, a
nightmurmur, Northern
Pacific

even empty
they carry
in dark corners
among smells of wood and sacking
the brown wrappings of sorrow
the persistence of war

and often
as they roll past
like weathered obedient
angels you can see
right through them
to yourself
in a bright
field, a crow
on either shoulder.

Three for the Moon

1

A bluegreen January dusk
and the full moon
risen
  beyond the water tower

Leaving the office
suddenly foolish with joy
I have one thought:
we don't
deserve
this earth.

2

Tonight the moon is not an onion
above a yellow Spanish town

or a fresh cabbage
over a Russian village

tonight the moon has one name
and no figure but its own

though my arm is more than an arm
my briefcase a sleepy farm.

3

Say it is dawn in the mountains
after the shortest night of summer
and I kneel at a pool
still in the shadows
watching the last four stars
rock slightly
                not winking out
but starting to join
the larger light

That is the feeling of the moon
as I drive home, flooding,
tumbling, part of the light
bright on the ice of the creek
round and fragrant in the pines

this water tower
looking glass
floodlight
moon!

Homing

1
"Attacks are being launched
to clean out enemy sanctuaries . . ."

Watching the president's features
I'm childlike
homesick.

For what?
A warm basement in Des Moines
a den in a thicket
the dense invisible pulsar
in the huge Crab Nebula . . .

2
The visiting poet
has been on the bottle
all over Ohio. Come back
to the state he was born in,
missing his wife and New York apartment,
he rolls his big flushed
baby's head and whispers
"I want my mother."

Unwilling to be left alone
unwilling to talk to us
he recites for a while like a bright child
and goes to bed hugging his misery.
Next morning he grabs a bus south.
I wave good-bye in the exhaust.
Everything's shaking.

3
The jackrabbit flushed by the car
is scared. In stiff

zigzag bounds he cuts
along the highway, then swerves suddenly
across an open field. Eighty yards to trees.
An easy shot.

But he knows
where he's going.

4
Pedaling home I glimpse
a sea-green boxcar
drifting along the tracks
by itself
and my uncle Bert, the best
farmer in the family
dressed in fresh overalls
clinging to the ladder
is he waving me off
or beckoning?

At dusk
a half dozen crows come
slowly over
the factory, the dairy
heading back
to their roost in the swamp
too far in
for hunters to follow.

In the yard
the smoke bush sings:
You have
nowhere to turn to
now.

5
Heavy and calm
summer rolls in
grass rises around us
like mother love
clouds build
in great treeshapes
yellow, peach, violet
disperse or crash in storms
and the trees, cloudlike
boil up in the wind
jittery, blazing green.

A black and yellow bird
—whose name escapes me—
startles me into pleasure
as I walk near the quarry
thinking of war, of the steady
state theory, of my children and
my parents, standing together
at Stonehenge
that Easter Sunday
my wife's mother
died of cancer.

Goldfinch! He flies up, wings
beating, is he in
my family, are we
home?

6
Sometimes I have to remember
to notice my children. Today

my daughter brought me a tulip
waxy and white, its petals
about to scatter—
hugging her I caught
in the fragrance of her hair
a smell of kinship.

Later we all
drove to the country
to see the green
sprouts in the long
plowed fields
the lambs, chickens, earthworms
who live so surely
on and in their earth, and when
we were tired
I glanced at the stacking clouds
and said
"Let's go home."

And we went
together, down the paved road
and not
as each of us would go
sometime, alone
rushing
across the black fields
toward the moon
that old bone
floating
out beyond evening.

May, 1970
Cambodia, Kent State, Jackson State

In Heaven

There
where the self is a fine powder
drifting free

simply by wishing
you can be
whatever you like:
a fish swiped by a bear's paw
a woman whose son is insane
a spear in the side of a tiger

They do not feast there
they do not hymn perfection or
the ecstasies of love

for their own reasons
they care most
to assume the shapes of suffering:

helicopters swooning into clearings
through crossfire, burning

or an old hare
limping across
a stripped field
in late November.

Mandelstam

"He had difficulty breathing. . . . Osip breathed heavily;
he was catching air with his lips."—Anna Akhmatova

1 *At the camp*

Hell freezing over. To keep sane
he studies the tiniest sensations
such as the touch of a necklace
of dry dead bees around a woman's neck.
Having said that, he can mention
honey, then speak of sunlight.
He studies his hands. Stalin's a swine.
Nadezhda's head is a beehive, full of poems.
He licks his lips to whisper one.
They're chapped. His breath is smoke.
His ears stick out as if to catch
even the noise of a candle flame.
Frostbite will get them first.
A sledge goes past, stacked high.
Better not look. Ice lies in piles,
shoals, hummocks. Memories of Warsaw,
Paris, Petersburg, the warm Crimea
keep their distance, northern lights,
or the swords of half-drunk cossacks
whirling through stupid dances.
He lives on garbage, is never warm, will die.

2 *The tear, 1938*

A tear is floating over Moscow
swollen, seeking a home, a mirror.

Tear, take my advice, get lost.
Those onion domes don't want you

the rivers are solid glass
the earth's a cake of permafrost

even those women wrapped in shawls
would gulp you like a drop of vodka.

Better go east, better follow
that long railway to Asia;

you can survive, little crystal,
in the glossy eye of a reindeer

on the bear's nose as he sleeps
dreaming sun into honey

in the fur of the wolf who runs
through the endless, falling snow.

3   *Nadezhda writes a letter*

Nonchalant, the sun goes off
and then returns. You won't.
Except in dreams, old films
flickering, buzzing when
your lips whisper, catching air,
making poems, sound tracks, and
I reach to touch you in the dark.

You left in a hurry, shrugging,
framed by policemen.
And your journey? The camps,
the cattle cars, beatings, stinks—
I see your forehead wrinkle, tongue thicken,
I turn away. Tears sting.
Maybe we should have jumped
hand in hand through the window!

It's warm in the Kremlin, there's music.
Stalin's small eyes glitter
his mustache is greasy with shashlik
he drinks, smashing his glass:
if the universe
makes any sense
how did we get from those fine-drawn
Petersburg afternoons
through the bonfires and rifle shots
of that marvelous revolution
to *this*?

But listen, Osip,
the joke's on them. Poems survive.
Your costly whispers carry.
They coexist with the state
like sunlight.
                    I can
still hear you, Osip;
catching air, your high-strung voice
speaks for the frozen and forgotten
saying, it *was* their earth, it was
their earth. Purges don't change that!

Though that's dim comfort tonight
as I sit with my bread and soup
and the wind off the wrinkled plains
howls like a man without a tongue.
Brave man, who shredded the death warrants
of a leather-jacketed terrorist
and then ran wild through the Russian cold,
my warm sun, shrunk to a star,
it's a stiff, black world
you left behind.

Thoughts of Chairman Mao

1
Holding black whips
the rulers rode
in the blue hills.

But the peasants were everywhere and nowhere,
a soft avalanche, gathering
courage; in famines
we ate the mules, tasting vinegar,
lived among rocks above the passes,
and gradually became an army
red flags snapping in the wind
and I wrote of "a forest of rifles,"
and of heroes strolling home
against a smoky
sunset.

2
Wars merge like seasons;
sometimes over hot wine
the old campaigners try to remember
who we were fighting that winter
on this plateau, that plain,
and whether we won.

It blurs . . .
miles in boxcars
doors wedged open
miles across blue-shadowed snow.
Hungry evening.

Artillery at the river
bodies in the rice fields
a black truck on its side
burning . . .

At night we could hear the gibbons
calling each other up the valley.
When there was a rest or a vista
someone would write a poem.
It blends and blurs:
conferences melonseeds sabotage
dungfires treaties mosquitoes
my great red army on the march
blinking in the sunshine.

3
Now it is changed.
I am the giant in the pageant,
toothy, androgynous, quilted.

To the slow roll of drums
my effigy speaks to the people
of harvests, steel mills, stars.

In the puppet shows I battle
enemies of the state
sometimes with blows and curses
sometimes with love and flowers
while Marx pops up to hug me
and Lenin takes my arm.

I would have done it
with poems! Instead
I have come to be
a red book, a pumped-up myth,
from Long March to Big Swim
surfacing, always surfacing:

said to have gone
miles through golden water
wrestled the Yangtze and won,
water god, flower king, rice prince;

the current takes me on
and it is no small thing
riding these tides, wave upon
wave of love, smiling, unspeaking,
ten thousand miles of mountains and water,
a chanting race, a skin on history,

until the people rise and go,
dispersing me.

4
At the end I enter a small room.

Stalin is standing there alone
hands behind his back
gazing out the window.

We link arms. We merge.

And the rulers ride the blue hills
holding their black whips high.

Ohio

Looking across a field
at a stand of trees
—more than a windbreak
less than a forest—
is pretty much all
the view we have

in summer it's lush
in winter it gets
down to two or
three tones   for
variety
there might be
an unpainted barn
water patches
a transmission tower

yet there's a lot
to see
        you could sit
all day on the rusty
seat of a harrow

with that view before you
and all the sorrows
this earth has seen
sees now   will see
could pass through
you like a long
mad bolt of lightning
leaving you drained
and shaken
still
at dusk
the field would be
the same and the growing
shadows of the trees
would cross it toward you
until you rose   your heart
pounding with joy and walked
gladly through the weeds
and toward the trees

Love Song

for Chloe

I guess your beauty doesn't
bother you, you wear it easy
and walk across the driveway
so casual and right it makes
my heart weigh twenty pounds
as I back out and wave
thinking She's my summer
peaches, corn, long moondawn dusks
watermelons chilling in a tub
of ice and water: mirrored there
the great midsummer sky
rolling with clouds and treetops
and down by the lake
the wild canaries
swinging on the horsemint
all morning long.

Chromos

1

Why have I pinned this postcard up?

Orange flames lick
the volcano's purple rim
under a plum-blue sky.

Wow.
I picture your face and breasts
lit by that glow. I decide
we will visit Hawaii.

2

Like a strange church the jet
sits in silhouette
under a dark grape dawn.

The runway looks deserted;
maybe the pilot, yawning,
is climbing into his harness.

At the horizon a wild
incandescence, yellow-white

as if the world was starting to burn.

3

In a slate-green night the lighthouse
pokes its beam at a right
angle to itself.

The beam looks solid
a dowel, a tube
a flattering self-portrait
of the lighthouse.

4

    The sky is navy blue
    the Flatiron Building's a handsome
    reddish-brown, speckled
    with tiny yellow squares.

    A lemon on a divan, the moon
    watches from puffy clouds
    thinking trout? basket? lightship?

5

What I want to do
is fan out a handful
of new cards, dazzlers.
Take a card:

    Geysers of light
    that mate around cities

    Mountains waxed and polished

    A picture of the well
    in the bottom of the sky

    The gears of light toward which
    we fall so gently as they knit

    The blades, teardrops, sphincters
    of lampshine

It's our appetite for light, it's how
the world keeps pushing back
the world we must invent,
all that give and take. . . .
Take a card:

    Those places I hoped to live:
    the Residence of Dorothy Lamour,
    Ethel Farley's Inn, the Willow
    Banks Hotel, and most of all,
    the Golden Temple of Jehol,
    are ablaze, blooming, collapsing . . .

By their light I can just
make out this postcard
this chromolithograph
this poem.

Notes on the Poems

1

Was found in an orchard;
is three or four thousand years old;
was probably made with poor tools
by the light of an oil lamp throwing
shadows against the wall
that would frighten us now.

2

Would never have been possible without
that famous fog of December 9th
for out of that fog came Geraldine
wearing a dress of chipmunk furze
with a grackle perched on her wrist.

3

Whole families were involved here
and the death wish and the industrial
revolution. You say the third line
about the bathroom in the grocery
was troublesome; I ask,
should a poem make more sense than Omaha?

4
It is right, little poem about
wandering and misunderstanding
that you kept coming back, unwanted.
Small avalanche,
always missing your victims,
come here—
I open my arms.

5
Of course the opening stanza
is like a cheap decal
of roses and tulips
on the side of a laundry hamper.
But as the poem progresses
you see something crawling
from one of the flowers.
An insect? Bend closer.
It is a very small man, holding a flashlight.
He snaps it on and swings the beam toward you.
You are blinded.

A Calendar: The Beautiful Names of the Months

January
On this yearly journey two
faces are better—a weary
woman, a wary man.

February
Where the earth goes
to run a fever. The care's good.
Herbs brew. The rooms are airy.

March
Bridge curving over a swamp.
A bruise that smarts, the long
patience of an army.

April
Neither grape nor apple.
Any monkey, a pearly sprig,
a prism. Flute notes.

May
The arch opens. Crowds.
Goats, babies, vowels and
the wind, permitting anything.

June
A jury rises.
The moons of Jupiter
set. Bugs, berries, prairie grass.

July
Jewelers snooze on the grass,
one eye open for the tall
constellation-poppies.

August
Clearing your throat of dust.
Wading in lagoons . . . algae,
hot bursts of wind.

September
Lives away from his brothers,
gentle-tempered, a little solemn.
Bears pests, eats peas and beans.

October
Cold roots and a fresh-caught owl
rocked on a cot.
An orange boot.

November
Toothache and memory.
Nine women. Overdressed beavers.
No new members.

December
Something decent, easy.
Frozen meekness. Wax. A good
end, an ember, then ten of them.

Teddy Roosevelt

Stumping again it hurts by god
have travelled all around the tattooed
lady my country looking for the right
spot to raise the banner of straw some
watertower some windmill though my big head
aches and i miss the waxworks greatly
clouds hang above old toads strange poppies
acetylene evenings seven fireflies solitude
blue pastures where a bull paws up cool soil
dragging my bad leg through the spirit village
seized by the women covered with sycamore leaves
as if i was the corn dog the potato man
no one knows me understands my language
the pulse of the tattooed lady is bad
i fear for her life i fear for her death
i would give her both if i could but i sit
here on the porch of this rainsmoke penthouse
where the music rises like mosquito smudge
through which a red sun comes rolling rolling

Woodrow Wilson

I pull on the tight clothes and go walking
rectitude misting around my figure
carrying the book of shadows a low moon
crosses the power stations the refineries
and in the needle mountains there are lakes
so cold and clear that the dead who sit
at the bottom in buggies and machine-gun nests
look up past the trout who nibble their shoulders
to see the eclipse begin the dime-sized shadow
sliding across the sun the insects settling
across the bears in their yokes the antelopes
acting out all their desires old lady
who smothers her young in her iron robes
you have wrung my thin neck a thousand times
and taken my pinch-nose glasses but
I come back again with the gliding Indians
settlers who have forgiven all their tools
the shabby buffaloes wild sheep wapiti
the inland sea that looks at the sky all day
with only a widgeon's wake to disturb it
the V dividing away from itself
all night under trembling constellations

from *Water Diary*

walking the tracks in early March
thinking where would I store a handcar
we ponder the fast clouds my son and I
and stare at winter's house   look down:
smashed grass gravel in a pool rainrings
wet rust on the tracks the creek rushing
no trains today no setting out arriving
the wind bucketing off through the trees
and sunset a skin of ice on each red puddle

~

my eyes heavy   the plumtree burning
muscles in my neck twist and I
reach toward you   even in summer air
your face is cool   a winter window
steelwork   we drive off the city lies
in haze behind but this
hot mist is everywhere
unsketching the little towns
and the fields with their cows and flies

~

the punt bumps the bank
jump ashore kick the boat back
to circle in the current
the black cinders crunch
here's the cottage the old man
sleeps at his desk everything's
familiar the blue door the sweater
over a chair the picture of a glacier
the ginger beer the Luger on the rug
the wind breathing in the fireplace
wells cisterns rainwater
lady lady lady lady

~

o stiff cadets your buttons shine
the rows of corn the aimed November wind
ran over a black snake near the quarry
going the wrong direction the daylight
racing across the clouds the dusty city
where a whole brass band got lost on purpose
or the sky where long blue moving vans
park to study aviation and the stars
what do you know about river currents
wheat sperm fountain lions drill towers
what it means to be human stop it at once

~

these lemons are packed in ice
then shipped to skating rinks in the Dakotas
or imagine a river of very chilly whiskey
lumber barons along the banks
we have all seen helicopters flying sideways
data-processing centers in Tennessee
astrakhan collars rain pocking snow
every direction is good and today
it has something to do with the cedar waxwing
seen at the feeder while I read Shakespeare
like starting over in the arms of water
"your body finds naturally its liberty"

~

the Empress seized the throne by unsavory means
and the poets strolled morose in the cashew orchards
young men were ridiculed by the thistle gate
while purple swallows flew in the snowy foothills
it is all the same   time   all the same
"Who now remembers," mused the Secretary of Rituals
"the monkey chariots that drew the courtesans
among the jade fountains and the pruned bamboo?"

and as he spoke, gazing out at his pepper plants
the invention of movable type occurred
and the waters of immortality faded from view

~

the olive-colored water spoke again
'49 Packards drew up to the Turkey Shoot
The Autobiography of Honolulu   listen
the water spoke volumes and the fruit
carved by the light of mutton tallow
made a perfectly good prize for the best
drop of water sliding down the cheek
imagine all this as a sort of waterclock
though not the kind that drips or burns
rising the months rising the mist rising
the spirits rising the mountains rising
meadowlarks constellations words

~

water is beads on the eaves steam
from a manhole cover most of my body
tears saliva urine sweat meadows flooding
what the spinning windmill pumps what
rains and bounces on mountainslopes
sinks into darkening earth is lost
and found again in giant summer clouds
shapechanger fog where glacier meets ocean
yesterday dew all over the freight car
rime frost today swamp pools tomorrow
imagination colorless and holding every color
window and mirror holding any image
the green creek wrinkling with a mallard
settling toward its own reflection in the sky
is time as line as circle is the snowman sinking
back inside himself is what can't be named is water

~

wrinkle wrinkle movie star the ice bird sang
she put her marvelous foot on the next step down
and shock waves traveled the length of her body
at the banquet there was a swan made out of ice
and several people dreamed of riding it naked
into that distance where light is no longer king
and nothing moves in the endless black lagoons
but darkness itself with a faint and dangerous slopping

~

for several days the temperature stood so low
that at last we could walk on water   and we did
the creek creaked softly talking to itself
along the banks through harmless fissures
we brushed some snow aside and peered down through
but could see nothing not water not even ourselves
there was a strange sensation of wrinkles and darkness
we knocked on the stuff   for entrance   for luck
and an old man spoke from a book
"why can't mind and matter
be more like wind and water?"
we looked up   snow was wobbling toward us
through miles and miles and miles of soundless air

from

Work Lights:
Thirty-two
Prose
Poems

1977

The Poem against the Horizon

In a dim room above the freightyards, next to an old brass bed, an angel is taking off his wings. He winces a little as he eases the straps that run down into his chest; the beat of the wings is the beat of the heart.

Out of harness, the heart rolls over now. Panting like a wrestler. Such love, such soaring! Spokane and back. So good to come down, home to this room with the stained lace curtains and the sound of switch engines. So good to remove the wings, the love, the yoke the blood must wear as it paces, oxlike, the circle of its day . . .

He sleeps on his side in the overalls he was too tired to take off. Outside the window, rain runs and drips from the eaves. Overhead, the wind and the black sky belong to someone else.

Four about the Letter P

Ponies grazing where there's wild garlic. "Only those who have smelled the breath of cows pasturing . . ." Thirty-four electric shock treatments. Fifty comas. Dances of women while men are away fighting. Whistling. Bumblebees around the salt. Scolding. While snow billows and blows through the orchards and windbreaks of the family farm, he moves quietly through the house, smearing blood on the walls and doorposts.

*

Let's say a white peony. In a jar. Water. Evening and the moon rising like a great engraving. No, like the face of a sleeper. That's better. The housewife peeking out through her curtain while I ring her doorbell. We have to feed ourselves. Ants, snails. We have to move around, even if the feeling we get is of wandering through a cold cathedral where we know we will encounter the face of the sleeper we are not allowed to photograph or describe. "Julie and her mother were at this time desperate people." Hear the bells. Open your eyes. It's the face, it's just the peony. Petals dropping on the polished rosewood.

*

Hauling a cake of ice from the icehouse, hosing off the sawdust, shaving it to slush that is packed around the can and dasher and sprinkled with rock salt, taking turns with the crank, doing this every Sunday morning through a whole summer so that some hundred people may have ice cream with chokecherry sauce, and never once thinking "This is a piece of the river."

*

How are the potatoes doing? From the field where you have come to inspect them, you can see the lights of the farmhouse not far off. Getting old, you think. Getting cold. Swear on this stone you will not steal yams. Thunder brings them to the surface. Long pigs run loose through the woods. The police can chase them. We sit on a verandah, sipping punch. "Magic," the psychiatrist says, "is contagious." Someone snorts. Soft moss, and the sound of a river. And pigeons, rose-gray like the winter woods, rising up startled.

Four about Heavy Machinery

A huge cement truck turns the corner, and you get the full impact of its sensuality. Those ruts in the road or on the lawn! Even at night the cement plant has a strange energy, drawing adolescents to stare through its fences, causing the watchman to shine his light nervously among the parked and sleeping mixers. Still, from those fluid beginnings and slow revolutions, the cement itself forms the pale and stony squares of sidewalk. Reassuring. Roller skates, hopscotch, salted ice. Then the slow cracking from the tree roots below and we are back to sensuality again.

*

Cranes are not to be compared with trees, not with their almost Scandinavian sense of the importance of power and duty. Sometimes the face is very far from the heart, and the one thing you would like to do—lie down next to that beautiful passing stranger, for instance—is the thing that seems least possible. So you sway against the gray sky, pretending to a stiffness you do not feel. The building you helped create rises toward you, filled with the sounds of hammering and the strange shine of worklights.

*

To take some tutoring from pumps, I said. I was thinking about the windmill, that swaying, clanking lecturer. Slow cows come to drink from the tank. We filled it didn't we, harvesting water from weather, not by bringing it down from the sky like rain, but up from the earth like oil. Now, roll up your blue sleeve and plunge your arm into that tank. If you clench and unclench your fist regularly you can learn something about the submersible pump, beating down there where weather is a dream.

*

We have strong feelings about bulldozers, their buzzing and scraping, their clumsy abruptness, their way of tipping saplings into piles of burnable roots and brush. Our faces get vinegary when we think of it. But the bulldozer's point of view is remarkably different. The bulldozer thinks of itself as a lover. It considers that its loved one, from whom it is always separated, is wrapped in many short, soft, buttery strips of leather. It imagines itself removing these worn leather wrappings, one at a time and with great tenderness, to get at the body of the loved one. Perverse, you will say. But see, you have already entered the life of the bulldozer: your hands reach for the next piece of leather. Shrubs and young trees go under.

Four about Death

Naturally, no one has been more misrepresented. The large dark eyes, for instance, with their penetrating glance. In fact, they are blind. But if you put your own up close to them, you begin to glimpse the many things within: the lovers in their squirrel cage, the panel discussion, the feast of the green-gowned goats, the bull's-eye lanterns strung through coastal villages. "So that is the sort of thing," you muse, "that lies beyond." The answer to that: not necessarily.

*

Rented the house next to mine. Aloof at first, seen occasionally clipping the hedge or putting out rabbit poison. Friendly waves as our carts passed in the grocery. Now and then limousines in the driveway, late lights, soft bell music. Thick red hair, golden beard, long fingers. When I realized he was spying on me, he confessed immediately, face ablaze. We discussed his loneliness and reached an understanding: weekly visit for tea and backgammon. We also exchange books, amidst disconcerting hints of greater intimacy to come. Something in that firm handshake makes me think I was wrong to take pity on him.

*

Peyote, no hot water, a relaxed attitude about magic—the American Indians got to know her extremely well. An Indian child could go sit with Death and chat. Such conversations tended to be dominated by her opinions. She considered the Cheyennes "autograph-seekers." She called the Aztecs a name that translates roughly as "The Heavies." About the Pawnees: "It's ridiculous, all those stories about Beaver Woman this and Buzzard Man that." As for the Navajos, she resented their interest in her relation to darkness, mosquitoes, intoxication, and travel. Her comments suggest a gruff affection. Which was reciprocated. Often. And with considerable taste.

*

I get your instructions in a letter. A small plane drops me at an airfield in the Andes. I stand by a rusting hangar, watching it climb out of sight. No one's around. Farther up the mountain animals I have never seen are grazing. Higher still a few clouds, resting against rocks. You do not arrive when I do. I must live in a hut for an undetermined space of time. Now and then I walk down to the village, carrying a basket for food and a jug for wine, but such things interest me less and less. Night storms light the mountains with blue flashes and send gusts of wind and rain that flatten the meadows. The morning of your arrival, I see a hare raised up, watching me. I do not know if you will come down the mountain or, more slowly, from below. All I know is that I will go out to meet you. My soul will be in my mouth.

Four about Mummies

Just one pause, in the sane and sleepy museum, is enough. You see the box, with its lid askew, the bone among ancient rags, it dawns on you that the face is not a mask. Now you will be related to it all your life. It will meet you by starlight in the courtyards of sleeping cities. Dressing or undressing your body, you will remember that box, face, rags. And in the horror movies, as you watch its caricature strangle and abduct the foolish archeologists, your smile will tighten and then vanish.

*

In the doctor's office there is a chart of the circulatory system. A blue-and-red thicket grows, but the figure it inhabits is otherwise white and blank; and the hands are spread, as if imploring. But communication is next to impossible. It is said that they have their own language, a compound of muffled odors in which they converse like birds. If you were patient and had a keen enough nose, a dark pyramid would be filled with a melancholy, spicy twittering.

*

Egypt's national pastime, given its history, skill, and climate. But we must not forget other nations. Some will have heard of certain North and South American Indian practices. A few may at least have an inkling of the Irish mummies, safe in their cradles of peat. But what of the Russian mummies, famous in their lifetimes as hypochondriacs? Or the Tartar mummies, poised against the horizon on their petrified steeds? Nomads who follow migrations must leave even their dying behind, but the rare, accidental mummies of the Lapps somehow contrive to keep up with the reindeer, and are sometimes even seen leading the vast, milling herds across the spring-washed tundra.

*

The body of the loved one, yes, tears and tar, to soak it, to wrap it, removing each organ except the heart, to fill the cavity with spices, to wrap each organ carefully and return it, to swaddle, to bandage, to blur. Does any happiness exceed this? Recall the simple pleasure of draping a shawl around someone's shoulders. And then the box: the façade, the mirror that dignifies, gaily painted, a boat, a boot, a gorgeous wooden nightgown. All of it to be stowed in the dark where even the explorer's torch cannot reach. There, in perfect silence, with the wrapped cat, the mummied hawk, the dishes of preserved food. Don't dismiss it: *only a fool or a god would shut the book of the dead.*

Kohoutek

In a broad field on a clear night you might stare at the sky quite uselessly, and with expanding dismay. I had the luck to encounter the comet on a gray morning when I was doing next to nothing in an upstairs room. I may have been restless and shaky, but my attention was steady as a trout. Outside, the plane trees began to stir. Then the mirror gave a small tremor. The comet was in the closet. Shaggy and silent. I glanced outside. The same pigeons were walking on the brown corrugated roof next to a skylight. But for a few fine moments, all the terrifying diffuseness—of matter, of winter light, of interest and love, of the Great Plains and the galaxies themselves—was just exactly bearable!

IV

from

The Names
of a
Hare
in English

1979

Two Views of the Cathedral

1. *Day*

Shoulder stones, blockstacks, peaks:
we put it up to catch our breath.
Thumbs, antlers, ferns and flying bones:
we put it up to catch the light.
A million thorns to house a rose,
another mask for god. And then a mind
hushed for the few thin sounds of dream:
the knicker-knack of pigeons in the frieze
the lunk of something closing in the crypt,
while a woman folds a large white cloth
in the wet yard behind the apse.

2. *Night*

Uneven candle crescent round the Virgin.
Casket time. The verger sees his breath.
High in the nave, the hunchback sees it all:
history is a slow march down the aisle, is
the countess sobbing in her heavy cloak.
Here a knight sat and felt his throat
fill up with blood. A crunch under my boot.
frost? mortar? salt? I tip my forehead back:
no roof, just dusty stars above . . .
We build. On the numb stone called fear
we fit the heavy one called love.

Nineteen Forty-four

Dragging a rake, my uncle Donald
surveys his Victory Garden:

peaceful and green,
all Minneapolis is at war . . .

since I am seven, that's mostly
cereal-box Messerschmitts,
Tojo cartoons, the bombers I draw
sailing through popcorn flak,
bad dreams, brownouts,

and the small cigarette machine
my father and Donald roll smokes with
as they sit up to grumble
at Roosevelt, winning again . . .

Countries of silence. Hand on my heart
I moon to return, searching for signs,
gnats in November, submarines
at rest on the harbor floor.

Then all at once I have done it!
I stand on the corner of Queen Street.
Five o'clock. The nations of the dead.
Mr. Kipke is whistling for his cat
and a light shines across the street
in the bedroom of the boy
with the bullet-shattered spine.

I sidle, thrilled, down our alley,
floating, loose as a ghost.
At our picket gate I find
my father, his back to me.
Is he pondering the war
or my brother, soon to be born?
I could touch his shoulder and ask him
but both of us are fading
as the city shines, all mystery,
and the garden sits empty in twilight:
pine needles, vines, brown leaves,
simple American shadows.

"Other Forms Were Near": Five Words

HONEYGUT (a word for tripe)

Below the graded greens of tree, bush, weeds,
it's silent—barn-cathedrals of quiet, but
no space: rooms all wall, jam-packed with roots (white sprays,
hard tentacles), pebbles, sand grains, humus,
tiger-striped tons of rock, pods of water and gas . . .

When you wake in the morning, rumpled and stunned,
the crumbs around your eyes are there to tell you
where you were lying all night, what you were practicing.

OAT

Yeats stands near his old-hat tower in the twilight;
everything talks to itself—the river over its rocks, the moorhens,
cricket and cowbell, wind in the chimney flue. What he's gaping at:
the Great Pyramid, trembling like a bubble above the trees.

"Willie is booming and buzzing like a bumblebee,"
said Maud Gonne to a friend. "That means he is writing something."
Who can he talk to when he's neither here nor there? Mumbling,
gaping. As the specters billow and fade. Ripe mummy wheat.

BABOON

Today a summer thundershower makes her think
of packs of sacred apes. Long hair, a kind of skidding run.
Isn't the animal mirror best? Those hours in the zoo
watching the young gorilla's hands: black leather work gloves.

The trees drip very strangely.
A robin runs across the lawn.

Bright eye.   Serpent mound.
The breathing next to your ear.

HAZE

Old, you were dozing at a window and woke up.
A stranger stood in the yard, the moon behind him,
so that you couldn't see his face. Then you recalled

watching a kingfisher from a canal boat: it was as if
that blue pulse tore straight through you. We're best

when the world shines us through like that. At night,
knee-deep in mist, the traveler pauses at a cottage
straining to catch his face in the empty casement.

INSECT

Cow skull, washtub. Sunday-supplement portrait. Gloomy greatness.
The poem's place in the world was "never in dispute,"
they said. Any more than a blizzard. Or a candle.

When the dead walk, do they need to use their feet?
How gradual it seems, going to sleep each night,
instar after instar. I pace my study, looking for a book.
The snowstorm settles in its globe. The small bright flame
is nearly independent of its wick.

How Music Began

Well, the wind blew so hard
that the sea blistered and snapped.
Even the boulders were squeaking.

Trolls scuffled and spat, whacking thick
bones on hollow oaks, screaming for meat,
and birds nattered in every thicket.

Women in birth-pangs howled. Bitter couples
shattered cups, jugs and beakers, while children
slithered on ice among grit and cinders.

*

Then thunder set off the landslide.
Bushes with dead birds tumbled
through blasted air. You couldn't hear

how bones and trees were splintered,
how boulders struck sparks, how the ice
burst, taking some of the children.

*

Then quiet grew up. Like cave pools,
cocoons. Like very old temples at noon.
Nursing. Fruitfall. Sketching the buffalo.

And then it was easy to consider
smoke a bird twisting up
that might sing as the earth got smaller.

Three Time-Trips

1
My shoes crush acorns.
I'm thirty-nine I'm seven.
Far down the yard
my father and a neighbor
sail horseshoes through the air.

The clank and settle.

And the past I thought would dwindle
arcs back to me, a hoop.

The men wipe their necks,
the boy walks round the oak:
sometimes our lives rust gently,
a long-handled shovel, leaned
against a sun-warmed wall.

2
Fourteen, I perch on the wicker seat
in a nimbus of misery, love's shrimp,
hearing the streetcar's crackle and hiss
as the drugstore turns on its corner.

And what was real? The whipped sparks,
the glove puppets, bobbing, the pocket dreams,
this poem-to-be, my father's wharf
of set belief, the wicker and shellac?

Learning to be imperfect—
that's erudition!
Like coolies in flooded fields
we wade on our own reflections.

3
November bleach and brownout. Acid sky,
falsetto sunlight, wire and fluff of weeds, pods,
bone and paper grass clumps. The dog bounds off,
stitching the field with her nose. Hound city.

It's thirteen years. Different dog, same field,
and double grief: dull for the slumped president
stake-sharp for my friend's ripped heart—faint
night cries in the mansions where we lived.

But the bullet grooves are gone, the first dog's dead,
and here is the field, seedy and full of sameness.
Speech fails, years wrinkle. Dream covers dream

that covered dream. My head starts up a jazz
I never could concoct. I have to grin. On the cold pond
the tinsmith wind is whistling at his work.

The Day Nabokov Died

1

I looked up from my weeding
and saw a butterfly, coal black,
floating across Plum Creek. Which facts
are laced with lies: it was another day,
it was a monarch—if it was black,
it must have been incinerator fluff.

A black hinge, opening and shutting.

2

Elsewhere the sunset lights
bonfires in hotel windows, gilds the lake,
picks out false embers where it can:
watch crystal, drinking glass, earring.
"Nabokov," someone calls, "is dead. . . ."
What would you give to be in, say, Fialta,
hearing the rhythms of a torpid coast?
Or on the porch at the Enchanted Hunters,
conversing in the shadows with Sirin?
Sneezes, lachrymose sighs. Chuckles and coughs.
When at a loss for words, try waving
one helpless hand before your face.

Walking the dog, I saw a hawkmoth too,
big as two hands, resting under a streetlight.

3

In the skyscraper across the lane
an aproned man sets up his easel
at the window opposite and cocks his head.
What does he see? A dwarf
mixing a violet powder, a fat
landlady playing patience, a little girl
brushing a velvet coat, in tears,
three people having sex. In short,
the world. Ourselves. Aren't all of us
some form of Maxwell's Demon,
particle sorters, systems
so self-enclosed they work too well to work?

Grandmaster, slip into your fiction like
Houdini diving through a pocket mirror.
Here's wonder, but no grief. And even so,
you'd not have liked this poem. Wan child
in a sailor suit, man running by
waving a gauzy net, tall fencer, pedant,
hotel mensch, empty suit of clothes . . .

One exile more. One language still to learn.

The Picture Says

1

That we all die, sometimes
when we are children.

That it would look like sleep
if flesh did not decay.

That we are marble, mottled,
that we are piebald clouds.

That we lie in the long grass,
peaceful, hair a little tangled,

grass like wires, spindles, rims,
grass like crisscross lifelines,

paths of the shooting stars,
arcs on the flecked night sky.

2

Sound of a backhoe, tractor-chug:
this old man is the pond digger—

he stands by the water's edge
on his open palm a pond snail . . .

he is humming, a kind of bee-speech,
while the child sleeps in the grass

the water a grainy mirror,
the light, the smoky lilies,

and the sky, filling slowly
with bruise-blue rain clouds.

Jaywalker

His arm leaves a dent in my hood.

He lies on the pavement, smiling
to reassure me.
                    Weeks later
the leak in his brain begins.
I try to imagine his headaches,
the murmuring nurses, the priest.
By then he is dead.

                    *

Twenty-two years. I can't
remember his face or name.
He came from a farm across the river.
We tried to visit his father and mother.

Tonight it's as though
my brakes have failed
and I roll through the hushed sirens
past white faces, past
the weary Night Dispatcher, steering
my old, slow Mercury toward
the figure across the river,
the boy from the empty farmhouse
with his smile, his trick headaches.

I would like to light him a candle.
I would like to bring him a drink of water.
I would like to yield the right of way.
I would like to call across the river.

"It's all right now?" I'd shout.

His head would bob in the wind.

Tool Talk

Put tip of pot through loop. Pull tight.
Call this position B. File flash and sand.
Use adze to strike off wobbly-pump
of Handley-Page or Spad. Dry roller stocks,
make notch in carrick bits with extra pick
and fit in spindle bush. Dash for the churn,
dash for the peak. Lakes equal paddles, bridles
are for camels, skies, a harness punch will fix
my son's new watch or fill that ladle in the stable.
Fit pitching chisel into granite crotch: release.
If cannon diagram does not apply, destroy.
Let sun god slide through threading lathe. Tie
lightning rod with thong. Work cork in slots of loom.
Rewind. Let sonnet slide from side to side.

After My Death

1

It will all go backward. Leaves
that fell in October will float up
and gather in trees for greening.
The fire I built will pull
its smoke back in while the logs
blaze and grow whole. Lost hailstones
will freeze themselves back into beads,
bounce once and rise up in a storm,
and as flowers unwilt and then tighten to buds
and the sun goes back to where it rose
I will step out through shrinking grass
at one for the first time
with my own breath, the wax
and wane of moon, dewsoak, tidewheel,
the kiss of puddle and star.

2

It will all go on. Rime frost, mist;
at the cracked mirror the janitor
will comb his hair and hum, three boys
will build a raft, chalk dust will settle
in blackboard troughs, trucks bump
on the railroad crossing, soft talk in trees,
a girl practicing her fiddle: I know this,
I keep imagining it, or trying, and sometimes
when I try hard, it is a small stone fern
delicate, changeless, heavy in my hand.
And then it weighs nothing
and then it is green
and everything is breathing.

A Lowercase Alphabet

a   snail going up the wall

b   hang up the little dipper

c   mouth, moon, river bend

d   the dipper in the mirror

e   tiny eye of the whale

f   oil well, skate, old pistol

g   what did you do to your glasses?

h   a chimney for every hut

i   the levitation of the spot

j   landscape with fishhook and planet

k   where three roads almost meet

l   romance of the periscope

m   comb from the iron age

n   the hut that lost its chimney

o   simplification of the blood

p   the dipper dead and buried

q   its mirror buried with it

r   geyser that goes off crooked

s   little black love seat

t   the portable cross

u   cross section of a trough

v   the hawk above the valley

w   a graph for winter, pig's foot

y   the root begins to sprout

z   path of the rabbit

from *The Names of a Hare in English*

Les Nouns de un levre en Engleis

The mon that the hare i-met
Ne shal him nevere be the bet,
Bot if he lei down on londe
That he bereth in his honde,
(Be hit staf, be hit bouwe),
And blesce him with his helbowe.
And mid wel goed devosioun
He shall saien on oreisoun
In the worshipe of the hare
Thenne mai he wel fare.

"The hare, the scotart,
The bigge, the bouchart,
The scotewine, the skikart,
The turpin, the tirart,
The wei-bitere, the ballart,
The go-bi-dich, the soillart,
The wimount, the babbart,
The stele-awai, the momelart,
The evil-i-met, the babbart,
The scot, the deubert,
The gras-bitere, the goibert,
The late-at-hom, the swikebert,
The frendlese, the wodecat,
The brodlokere, the bromkat,
The purblinde, the fursecat,
The louting, the westlokere,
The waldenlie, the sid-lokere,
And eke the roulekere;
The stobhert, the long-here,
The strau-der, the lekere
The wilde der, the lorkere,
The wint-swift, the sculkere,

The hare serd, the heg-roukere,
The deudinge, the deu-hoppere,
The sittere, the gras-hoppere,
The fitelfot, the foldsittere,
The ligtt-fot, the fernsittere,
The cawel-hert, the wortcroppere,
The go-bi-ground, the sitte-stille,
The pintail, the toure-tohille;
The cove-arise,
The make-agrise,
The wite-wombe,
The go-mit-lombe,
The choumbe, the chaulart,
The chiche, the couart,
The make-fare, the breke-forwart,
The fnattart, the pollart,
(His hei nome is srewart);
The hert with the letherene hornes,
The der that woneth in the cornes,
The der that alle men scornes,
The der that no-mon ne-dar nemmen."

When thou havest al this i-said,
Thenne is the hare migtt alaid.
Then migtt thou wenden forth,
Est and west, and south and north,
Wedrewardes so mon wile,
The man that con ani skile,
Have nou godne dai, sire hare!
God the lete so wel fare,
That thou come to me ded,
Other in cive, other in bred! Amen!

MS Digby 86f 168 v. (1272–1283)

I

Just an old poem. Beyond us,
worn as a bone—but this one
seems to keep doubling back.
Look: fresh tracks, a crosspath. Nervous,
I glance around. I want to know
who wrote it. What liar would claim
seventy-some names for
the pop-eyed, great-hearted
cousin of the rabbit?

I think I know what happened.
I get these fits myself.
For a moment language is everything,
a path to the heart, a small
city of stars on the tongue:
then everything looks in the mirror
and sees his cool twin nothing . . .
seventy names are none.

2

In the time before dawn, in graylight,
a fur purse hops through the soaked grass,
a stump stands by a stump and then is gone;
this is the time when names are none and many,
the time when names themselves have names.

Say the word, things happen.
Say the long hare is a deer, there's
a crash in the bracken. Say
fiddlefoot, you hear pounding
on the packed door of the earth.

Prospero stands in his sour ring
somebody else's fict. "Turpin,"
he whispers, and a small
furzecat appears at his feet.
"Dewbert," he says, and now
there are two, sidelookers,
late-at-homes, the master smiles,
says "Budget," there are four,
says "Hedgecroucher" and
there are eight but
you know how this
story comes out. . . .
What do we have for animal magic
but names, our mumbled spells and charms,
baskets of epithets spilled down the page?

A straw deer stood here
right at this line
but a grassbiter ate it
and then a broomcat swept it away
a windswift blew or flew to where
the westlooker stood looking east
toward the wastelooker in his hair
shirt, but
you know how this goes
you turn the corner of the line
and startle a fernsitter who evaporates
now you see him now
you don't now you name him now . . .

3
Along the Vermilion River
the farmer's wife points out some shallow caves
where slaves hid on the way to Canada
and Indians rested, migrating south.
Settlers stood on the bank and watched,
I figure, as I do, hands in my pockets,
wanting to belong to this, or it to me.

An old woman with us knows
the name of every plant.
"What's this?" I ask, testing her.
"Mary's bedstraw," she says!
I'm shivering. To know the name,
to possess and be possessed!
Don't apologize. Wild geranium, dog violet,
sneezewort, bloodroot, jack-in-the-pulpit,
so we trail through the river-bottom woods
and names bind us to strange forms of life.
A good new name, I tell myself,
is what the farmer feels, turning
an arrowhead or axehead up.
His hand closes around the past,
the mystery of why he's here;
the world extends too far
and yet he's in it, holding a small rock!

We pace on through the woods. Trillium everywhere,
stars on a green spring evening,
bones in an Irish pasture.

5

We have some quiet families in this neighborhood.
Constellations, let's start from there. Bear, Plough,
Charles's Wain, how choose? Pleiades: better
as Seven Sisters, but I like Hen and Chickens best.
Is that Pandora, lid-lifting? No, President Taft,
strolling with his cigar. Andromeda,
chained lady? How about Rita Hayworth's
Iceboat? Go on, make up your own,
holding a child's hand, saying: See, there's Moth.
Glove, Submarine. Malcolm's X.
Chandelier. Cottontail. Moebius Strip: God's Ring.

Well, drop your head.
The field's still here, with its milk vetch and thistles,
the house with its one lamp lit.

7

Shakespeare's portrait hangs in my office.
The round, poised face, balding and bone-yellow,
hovers on its ruff against
a dark brown background. Lately,
when I glance up it is
my father's face. And I am pleased. Afraid.
What the prince told the ghost flares a second
against brown sky: *I'll call thee . . . father.*

My father's alive and well
in Minneapolis. His business
was business, but the other day

he gazed at me from a dust jacket
in Wallace Stevens' look. That's dangerous,
that father-saying. A breath huffs, jaw drops,
tongue jumps between teeth. To say
I'll call, I'll call you, I'll call *you*
father. And call. And you. Then
they start to call you father. What a name.
A cloak, a jacket.
You take it off.
Your head floats off the ruff. Your gaze
travels. Your sons wince.

8

I look at the backs of my hands and get lost:
an old wind bends the grass, blue trails fan
from wrist to flushed and crosshatched knuckles;
stand on one, look out along
the five peninsulas, ridges crossed
by ravelins and runnels, at the tips
the slick nails flaring; you could do
a tap dance, smiling, and fall off. . . .

I look at my hands, searching for their names,
picker and stealer, Guildenstern and Rosencrantz,
the scarred serf who dropped the crystal goblets,
the oldest cups, the simplest maps,
furrow-makers, strangling partners, fist and claw,
smoothing the child's hair, poking shadows,
wringing laundry, helpless in sleep. I look
at my hands. How could they have names?

A day swings past. A husk of hares
disappears over the hill. Dawn again.
I've looked at the small change in my pocket:
eye, star, hand, rain,
father, mirror, bedstraw, bloodroot.
Now, doing my act, I find a bone,
step in the sour circle, find
the bone knows how to sing:

> "Folwes in the frith
>   The fisses in the flod,
> And I mon wax wod.
>   Mulch sorwe I walk with
> For best of bon and blood."

Fishes in the flood, and I could go mad:
language, that burrow, warren, camouflage,
language will deceive you and survive you.

Well then, so what?
I look up *frith*.

Oh, game preserve of metaphors!
Oh, goldfinch feeding in the buttonbush!
The dogs of death are loosed
upon that little word, that rabbit,
but he can double back. And does.

from

Foraging

1986

In My Own Back Yard

1

July, I'm dozing in sun on the deck,
one thrush is singing among the high trees,
and Li Po walks by, chanting a poem!
He is drunk, he smells unwashed,
I can see tiny lice in his hair,
and right through him
a brown leaf in the yard
flips over flips
again lies still
all this time
no wind.

2

From behind November glass I watch the wind
truck all its winter furnishings
item by item into my yard.
In a dusty raincoat my neighbor
throws a tennis ball, over and over,
to exercise his police dog.

Sometimes I feel like one of the world's bad headaches,
sometimes I think I get no closer
to what I have wanted to mean
than the gumshoe calling
"Testing"
up to the bugged ceiling. . . .

You can try to put words to a mood
or tell yourself to ignore it
but what kind of message is coming
from the chickadee, dapper
in his black mask and skullcap,
grooming himself on the big pine's branch-tip?

His music is small and monotonous,
but it's his own.

3
I am turning pages in lamplight.
Outside, above blue snow, in February dusk,
in the double world of glass,
more pages flip, like wings—
this merging of me and the world
done with mirrors and windows.

4
Hunting for duck eggs at the end of March
I watch three mallards and a speckled female make·
a tight flotilla on the swollen creek.

The dog barks at her counterpart
on the other bank. Nothing is green
the way these mallards' heads are green.

Empty-handed, I turn back to the house.
Small waterlights
play on the underbranches of the ash. High up
the sycamore lifts its light-peeled limbs
against a turning sky.

5
Late May. Summer coming on again. I think
Li Po may not be back. Worried about
the world's end, as, I realize,
I have been most of my life,
I take my work outside
and sit on the deck, distracted.
It was a day like this, I think,
in Hiroshima.
Distracted.
There must be something in the pinecones
that the chickadees—there's another one.
What's this that's snowing down? Husks, pollen,
freckle-sized petals from our wild-cherry trees!

We sneeze and plant tomatoes. Ultimatums. The world
comes close and goes away
in rhythms that our years
help us begin to understand.

We haven't long to live.
And the world? Surely the world . . .
A deep breath. Sunshine.
Mosquitoes, bird calls, petal hail.

A Ghost, to One Alive

There you sit, in the midst of your heart's rich tick,
your breath coming and going,
a lax and happy piston;

your eyes blink, your tongue slicks your lips,
your brain hums, gobbling oxygen.
Oh, hot unconscious life . . .

I know I am hard to imagine—
a smoke-bag, a spindle of mist, fume of an old fear-pot—
but you are just the opposite:

you ruin this sweet hush, two times too real,
and I find I have to drift back
from your clicks, wheezes and smells,

your mask of hope over a hopeless gape,
one eye on the wagging clock, muffled
amazement, bundle of hungers, oven stuffed with yourself!

If you knew a bit more, you might envy me,
moon-scalded as I am
voodoo-hooded and vague as cheesecloth,

a simulacrum of solid old you,
the last billow from a cold, closed furnace
a dimple, at best, in existence,

the birdcall without the bird.

Two Trips to Ireland

1
Well-eye, gazing at daytime stars,
rain-speckle, patches of blooming mists
a hillside white with water-spill
a shower blowing inland at the coast . . .

All this water must *mean* something!

2
Long deserted glens in the Wicklow Hills
and an axe buried in a tree so long
only the tip of the handle shows.

3
The small hotel in Gort, ale and roast lamb,
the midday drowse. Who breathed this air?
Who climbed these stairs? Time floats,
one face of a diamond, scraps of paper in the street.

4
From these ruined beehive huts
on the bright slope you can see
half the Dingle and
the distant winking sea.

Monks, who had to be
gone in the head.
Where's their god now?
Look closer at the cross-eyed pup
that followed you up this slant pasture,
the heifer that kneels, gazing out
on miles and miles of sun and rain-washed air.

5
And the wind, a mind that's never still,
with its black thoughts, the rooks at Cashel,
its white thoughts, the sea gulls at New Grange,
all this tossing and cawing among great ruins.

6
Lisadell: cracks, tatters, stains.
An old lady in gumboots
shepherds a handful of tourists;
from an upstairs window
you strain to see the past,
horses like swans, peacocks on gravel
cloudburst at four and dress for dinner . . .

Night fog. Ghosts in the garden,
ghosts on the stair,
ghost of an old fiddler, air threading the air.

7
On a back road by a tower
a movie crew, Arthurians lunching.
Why not? Time-levels mix like bones
in pasture-battlefield, bog-shrine.
Iseult still boils spuds for the pig
and Tristan, cutting turf, turns up
a Roman coin or a telephone cable.
That Viking ship below the Moher cliffs
is a film prop or another fold
in the wrinkled suit of time.

8
The river Fergus
runs like a wild clock
by the tumbledown house we rent
on a cold lake in County Clare.
Near the ruins of the mill
I catch an eel and, feeling a fool,
I let him go.
A local rod-and-tackle man
who comes and goes like a ghost in the dusk
says I could have kept him "for a pie"
then hints at what I ought to know:
the trout are far too smart
to let themselves be caught
by a man so trapped in time.

October Couplets

1

Again the cold: shot bolt, blue shackle,
oxalic acid bleaching a rubber cuff,

a cow-eyed giantess burning roots and brush,
the streak and smash of clouds, loud settling jays,

crows roosting closer—my older-by-one-year bones
have their own dull hum, a blues; it's all plod,

but they want to go on, above timberline,
to boulders, florets, ozone, then go free

in the old mill that the wind and the frost run
all day all night under the gauze and gaze of stars.

2

Somewhere between sperm cell and clam shell
this space cruiser takes me places I'd rather

stay clear of; a planet all graveyard, mowed,
graveled and paved, bride-light and parson-shade,

or a milkweed, bitter, about to burst, or a dropped
acorn even a squirrel didn't want, browning to black,

and I have to learn to relax with it all, to sing
"Where the bee sucks, there suck I," though the lily

is sticky and choking, bees don't suck, and the sting
is a greeting you never recover from.

3
"Steam of consciousness," a student's fluke,
makes me see a lake, linen-white at evening,

some amnesia-happy poet all curled up
sucking a rock at its black bottom;

oblivion tempts everyone but I
would miss too much—whales and ticks,

the weather's subtle bustle, blue crab clouds,
my kite rising, paper and sticks, a silver ember,

while the poem's ghost waits by the empty band shell,
does a little tango, taps out its own last line.

4
But this fall rain, somehow both thread and button,
sewing itself to the malachite grass,

beading the clubs and brushes of the spruce—
all day I have sat as if gazing over water,

wind feathering the reservoir, stupid as a church,
and thought of summer: all those burst horizons,

mineral cities, rosy meat, clean seas and shaggy islands,
the wine cork popping in the grape arbor,

these things seem better and clearer than gods just now,
raspberries hung like lamps among their brambles.

5

These leaves, these paper cutouts drifting the yard,
stars, fish, mittens, saddles: the badges and epaulets

of emptiness—last night in my dream
I was the killer, the guard who failed to stop him,

and the child who froze and was spared: Nothing lasts,
sang the crowd, and I answered, It sure does;

Is nothing sacred, roared the statesman—I do
believe it is, said I . . . I wake and shave,

still full of my dreamflood—oh, skim milk sky,
oh, brown star curling in my hand . . .

Basho

Tonight, on the other side of the lake,
someone is walking with a lantern.

The changing light on the water
— a blossom, a wasp, a blowfish —
calls me back from desolation
and makes me sigh with pleasure.

How can I be so foolish?

*

It's true! All night
I listen to the rain
dripping in a basin . . .
in the morning I have a haiku.
So what!

All these years
and I think I know
just about nothing:
a close-grained man
standing in haze by the warm lake
hearing the slap of oars
and sobbing.

*

For weeks now, months, a year,
I have been living here at Unreal Hut
trying to decide what delight means
and what to do with my loneliness.

Wearing a black robe,
weaving around like a bat . . .

                    *

Fallen persimmon, shriveled chestnut,
I see myself too clearly.

A poet named for a banana tree!

Some lines of my own come back:
Year after year
on the monkey's face—
a monkey mask.

I suppose I know what I want:
the calm of a wooden Buddha,
the state of mind of that monk
who forgot about the snow
even as he was sweeping it!

But I can't turn away from the world.
I sit and stare for hours at
a broken pot or a bruised peach.
An owl's call makes me dance.

I remember a renga we wrote
that had some lines by Boncho:
somebody dusts the ashes
from a grilled sardine. . . .
And that's the poem! That sardine!
And when it is, I feel
it is the whole world too.

But what does it mean
and how can it save you?
When my hut burned down
I stood there thinking,
"Homeless, we're all of us homeless. . . ."

Or all my travels, just so much
slogging around in the mire,
and all those haiku
squiggles of light in the water . . .

*

Poems change nothing, save nothing.

Should the pupil love
the blows of the teacher?

A storm is passing over.
Lightning, reflected in the lake
scares me and leaves me speechless.

I can't turn away from the world
but I can go lightly. . . .

Along the way small things
may still distract me:
a crescent moon, a farmer
digging for wild potatoes,
red pepper pods, a snapped chrysanthemum . . .

Love the teacher, hate the blows.

Standing in mist by the shore,
nothing much on my mind . . .

*

Wearing a black robe,
weaving around like a bat —
or crossing a wide field
wearing a cypress hat!

The Self: A Sonnet Sequence

I

If we are what we see, hear, handle,
then I am London now: rain light and chimney pots,
shuddering buses, streaky-bacon flat-blocks,
rooks in a queue. Reading your novel, I was a girl

who took up living in a barn. Sense-pestered,
trailing itself around the world,
the self is now and then complete as it locks in
to mingle with an afternoon, a page, a person. . . .

In the Siberian frozen tombs they found
wool socks, expressive faces, rugs, fresh leather,
a chieftain's arm still glowing with tattoos:

what the self freezes, what the self digs up—
what do you want to call it, kid?
Weather. A city on a page. A mirror.

2

Self as imperialist, pushing out his borders?
Oh, the ego rides in armor, bellows threats,
but his helmet's a pocked kettle, he'll turn tail
as soon as he sees the torches of the future,

he's far less real than, say, his horse's shoulder.
The anarchists he hired are dismantling
what's left of his soft palace, heaving chunks
into the swift and unbecoming river.

A candle: what it means to do is vanish,
brightly. The self: what it means to do
is make a candle. Something of that kind,

and the object — horseshoe, cabbage, poem—
is what the self just hoped to run together to
and fill: a cup of anonymity.

3
Well, no, not run together. Scatter: smoke
in its eloquent hoods and cowls. Clouds,
their race and rain. We're swarms of funny matter
(ice, rust, grasses, moonsparks, puff paste)

longing and fearing to disperse. "Can't get away
from you-know-who" (scratched on a mirror), but the eye
sees way beyond the eye, and the mooncalf mind
sits on its shelf and flies great kites.

"After the dancers have left
and the grand ballroom is empty,
the old beekeeper brings

a rustling and humming box;
and the band begins to play again,
but you've never heard the music."

4
My young self comes to see me, fresh and friendly.
He is from 1957, and anxious to get back.
I think he is just polite about my acting
as though we had lots in common. Stands in the doorway,

charming but rushed. I'm amazed
that I like him so much, like him at *all*,
he has such an air of self-discovery,
as if one day to the next he *knows* himself

(first love, acting, superficial poems),
a life he thinks I'm merely interrupting.
I live inside his dream, he inside mine,

and we back away from each other, smiling,
a couple of meadows, a couple of knives,
affection brimming between us as we go.

5
Is a pebble. Is a bubble. Drags its little sled
through empty salt flats under a cobalt sky
of nailed-up stars. Is a lamb with real sharp teeth,
a tongue waltzing in a moonlit clearing. Is

a donkey, leaning against a mulberry tree
in which the silkworms spin their mysteries;
hugs itself, hugs itself and cries,
a horn full of sparks, a shadow at a keyhole.

The critic wanted to enter the very brush stroke,
then find the brush, then climb the painter's arm,
muscle and vein and nerve to mind and heart:

instead he stumbled and then he was falling forever
through meaningless words that were falling too
in exactly the opposite direction.

6
Has it parents strapped on like backpacks,
grandparents in a suitcase; its orders are
to move the grand piano over a mountain
without upsetting the buckets of milk for its children.

The house is sheared open by the wrecking ball
and there is the bathroom, flashing its mirror,
the wallpaper, losing track of its pattern,
the chest of drawers where father kept his condoms.

Tear rolling down the hill of the corpse's
cheek. Big tear that rolls off the stiff blue chin.
Things left behind, trash bin and junkyard.

Rain won't be different from skin.
Eye won't be different from view.
Smoke will take root and every flower float.

7
Hyde, this Jekyll: no more rages,
no more rapes and stranglings. I leave this flat
only for necessary shopping.
On the horizon, the orphanage burns.

Evelyn Waugh, timid of ridicule,
built up a carapace so thick
he could hardly move inside it—except to write
painful, hilarious novels, ridiculing the world.

The daylight brightens, dims and brightens.
Late March. Atoms of nostalgia,
flakes of essential self. Crusoe on his beach

pondering a footprint. Still March. Outside
the blown rain writes nonsense on the windows,
the pear tree strains against its ivory buds.

8
One of those houses where the eyes of portraits move
and suits of armor mutter by the stairs.
But this was worse. The chairs had body heat
and every sink was specked with blood.

I swept from room to room, my cape
billowing out behind. Sat by the fire
poking the panting coals. Hid beneath a bed
and listened to them screwing in the attic.

Think of a liquid. Dog slobber. Cattle drool.
Dipped up in a leaf-cup from a spring. It's true
anything other than human could comfort me now

like that French poet who could put his face
against a hanging side of beef
and still his fear.

9
Good-bye to the night sky, the Milky Way
a bone-seam on a cranium, vein in a cave.
Now dawn is a rooster, noon a pheasant
crossing the road. I drive. Land's End, Tintagel,

the landscape fills me slowly, like a sail.
A daylight display, a wind off the Atlantic,
ego shadows sailing across pieced fields,
a herd of clouds without a shepherd.

Sometimes the world will fit you like a sweater
and you think ingenuity and fortitude
can see you through, your recipe and axis.

I have to say this clumsily; at best,
the image trembles in its instant, star
in a pail of water carried through a glade.

10
In Voronezh did Mandelstam
sing of his death the winter I was born
in Davenport, in Iowa, all mother's milk and love
against his sour tea and fear. The contrast

makes me wince. I want . . . to be a goldfinch too?
No, and I'm not the point. Nor Mandelstam. We're both
exhibits of the self, the flesh made word,
singing its own confusion and delight:

all this takes place despite the big world's Stalins.
I write this in the Royal Mail, in Islington.
"Hullo, Stanley," says the barmaid. Pool balls click,

the jukebox throbs. We bob on currents,
taking the world as best we can, each planet
cruising its dawns and dusks around the sun.

England. January–May 1979

Hunting for Mushrooms in Orange County

Like a snail on a cabbage leaf
I move along this hillside.

Blank eyeballs bulging in the grass,
doorknobs to darkness, night's white knuckles,
the scattered cups and saucers of the dead,
old smoky hard-ons coaxed up by the rain!

There are stars and flowers in this world,
green sprouts, plump nuts, threshed grain,
fruit in bright rinds and clusters—

but there are these buttons too,
these pallid lamps, lit by a secret,
tokens so strange we hold our breath to eat them,
puffball, campestris, morel,
wrinkled and chalky blebs of foam.

I look up from my gathering
and think I don't know where I am . . .
the buckskin hills, the instant cities,
this grainy earth we find and lose
and find again
and learn to say we shall lie down in,

meanwhile nibbling on these swollen caps
beautiful messages of decay, from roots, bones, teeth,
from coal and bark, humus and pulp and sperm,
muzzle-skull, channel and hand, the all-containing dead,

invisible branchings of our living smolder—
I glance around me, half-bewildered,
here in this California sunlight
spore dust drifting right through my body

a meadow mushroom humming between my fingers.

Suite for Jean Follain

1
In September there come to Ohio
clouds out of old Dutch paintings
above weeds in gold confusion
in overlooked orchards apples
drop in the wild grass
a baby strapped in a station wagon
stares at the checked jackets
of hunters stooping to gather
groceries spilled on the sidewalk.

2
Never came back to visit
says the old woman out loud
lugging a bucket of feed
across the empty farmyard
beyond her a shed is collapsing
terrifically slowly a cow
is chewing without expression
white stars pass
from a burst milkweed.

3
The evening has turned the blue
of a milk of magnesia bottle
and the big American flag
is snapping against itself
in front of the courthouse
looking up at the window
where she undressed he thinks
of wrens and tent revivals
and statues from ancient Egypt.

4
A wet stone beehive
stands in the middle of the garden
beyond the wall delivery trucks
occasionally pass
a smell of burning leaves
reminds the mailman of childhood
a fish jumps in the reservoir
in the graveyard clumps of honey mushrooms
blacken slowly in rain.

Elegy in the Form of an Invitation

*James Wright, b. 1927, Martin's Ferry, Ohio;
d. 1980, New York City*

Early spring in Ohio. Lines
of thunderstorms, quiet flares
on the southern horizon.
A doctor stares at his hands.
His friend the schoolmaster
plays helplessly with a thread.

I know you have put your voice aside
and entered something else.

I like to think you could come back here now
like a man returning to his body
after a long dream of pain and terror.

It wouldn't all be easy:
sometimes the wind blows birds
right off their wires and branches,
chemical wastes smolder on weedy sidings,
codgers and crones still starve in shacks
in the hills above Portsmouth and Welfare . . .
hobo, cathouse, slagheap, old mines
that never exhaust their veins—
it is all the way you said.

But there is this fierce green
and bean shoots poking through potting soil
and in a month or so the bees
will move like sparks among the roses.

And I like to think
the things that hurt won't hurt you any more
and that you will come back
in the spring, for the quiet,
the dark shine of grackles,
raccoon tracks by the river,
the moon's ghost in the afternoon,
and the black earth behind the plowing.

Vermont Summer: Three Snapshots, One Letter

Imaginary Polaroid

In this picture I am standing in a meadow
holding a list of fifty-one wildflowers.
It is Vermont, midsummer, clear morning
all the way to the Adirondacks.
I am, as usual, lost. Misplaced. But happy,
shaggy with dew. Waving my list.
The wind that blows the clouds across these mountains
has blown my ghosts away, and the sun
has flooded my world to the blinding-point.
There's nothing to do till galaxy-rise
but name and gather the wildflowers.
This is called "pearly everlasting."
And this one is arrow-leaved tearthumb!
Hawkweed, stitchwort, dogbane, meadow rue . . .
The dark comes on, the fireflies weave around me,
pearl and phosphor in the windy dark,
and still I am clutching my list,
saying "hop clover, fireweed, cinquefoil,"
as the Milky Way spreads like an anchor overhead.

Robert Frost's Cabin

He perched up here at the lip of the woods
summer after summer. Grafted his apple trees
into a state of confusion. Came down
two or three times a season to be lionized.
Mesmerized visitors with talk,
or hid from them. Or both.

Charles and I look in his windows.
There's the famous chair.
The place is tiny, but the view is good.
We shake our heads at his solitude.
Couldn't he have the kind of friendship
that brought us up here together?

How can we keep from becoming such molluscs?
Easy, says Charles. Don't live that long.

Hayhenge

After the meadow was mowed and before
the bales were gathered, the students
erected a midget Stonehenge in the moonlight.
It stood there all the next day:
real from a distance and up close
sweet-smelling and short-lived.

Off and on I've been pondering models:
I think they are all we have.
Snapshots, cabins, lists. Metonymies.
At Lascaux they've opened
a replica of the caves. I shall get
Peter Quince to write a ballad of this dream . . .
The sun goes down beyond Hayhenge;
clouds and mountains mix in the distance.

Letter to Chloe

Since you left, we've had
wild blackberries, northern lights,
and one grand thunderstorm.
Again, these mountains have been
Chinese with their graduated mist.
Tonight it's clear and we hope to see
a meteor shower. I'm teaching Vaughan,
who tried to show us another world
with images of light, and knew
he needed dark to make the light more real.

I shake my head, still lost.
I'm lucky if I find a berry,
name a flower, see a shooting star.
You and I cried a little at the airport:
each parting's a model for something bigger.
But I don't think our models mean much.
We try to take them as they come:
a trefoil in the hand, a meteor trail
crossing the retina, a black and glinting
tart-sweet berry in the mouth.

Three Walks

Near "Appleby," Axminster, Devon. June 1982

A path, a garden, a country lane
with a very old lady and her daughter,
the whole evening holding tremulous
as though it might never end.
A codger watering his broccoli
talks up the art of gardening as
we gaze at his cabbages and gooseberries.
By his garden wall and along the lane
foxglove is speechlessly in bloom,
herb Robert, hogweed, eglantine,
everything, even the grass and cuckoo-spittle,
touched with the slow welling up of life.
When we come back I hear again
some thrush in the deep shade
making music as intricate
as what we were walking through.

Near Arcidosso, Tuscany. July 1979

Maybe I like this city for being
nearly unknown, off in the mountains.
Over and over the cuckoo calls from the chestnuts
this sleepy midday. Red-and-lemon posters
for a circus, ORFEI, plaster every wall,
and I can imagine a humdrum Orpheus
ambling the narrow street to the bakery,
pausing to stare
at the round fountain where a stone mask
blows a thin rope of water
into a basin, a rope without ends.
He would climb to the old castle,
baking in sunshine, where
the air is alive with bees

that build in the crumbling masonry.
What would he make of it all? Would he stand,
his eyes blurring with tears,
looking back through the smoke of time
at the men and women, come and gone,
who have seen how the earth is lovely
and seen how its meanings desert them?

Near Lorain and Oberlin, Ohio. July 1982

Backward and forward in time, as if
by way of England and Italy I've come
to stand in the K-mart parking lot
while Cassiopeia hangs askew
beyond the cornfields, come to hear doves
calling all morning in the rain
like very tired cuckoos.
Tomorrow, the Fourth of July, I'll go
mushroom-gathering in the cemetery
to the rumble of summer thunder
among the distant dead, Huron Weed, Amanda Peabody,
and the newer dead I knew, George Lanyi, Jean Tufts,
and if it's not so time-caressed
still I will pause there, startled
as though I stood on my own heart
in nature's haunted house,
as again, in the long-drawn evening,
with the fireflies signaling—
commas, hyphens, exclamation marks—
and the skyrockets in the distance—
foxgloves, fountains, bees,
constellations and mushrooms
hung for a second or two
on the dim sky above the trees.

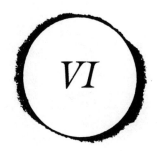

from

Earthshine

1988

The Moon-Globe

This small tin model of the moon
gift of a friend, tipped on its stand,
is one of the featured and featureless
things that survive you now.

It's mapped, but not in relief:
one can see and study, but not feel,
the craters and mountain ranges.
Sometimes I rub the missing wrinkles.

There's no dark side to this moon.
No light one either.
Just enough gloss to reflect
a smudge of daylight on its gray-blue surface.

I move it from desk to bedside,
giving my grief a little spin,
putting the surface, which ought to be rough,
against my shaved and moony cheek.

from *Nine Deaths*

"Cancer is a series of deaths."—Georgia Newman

1 *Surgery*

Late April. You've just learned
they will cut away your breast, or part of it.

We've cried,
discussed statistics,
told our children and friends. For relief
and a little privacy
we drive out
to West Road
south of the reservoir,
and walk in the green spring evening
hearing cows and birds, watching leafing trees.

"The world's so beautiful," I say. Or is that you?
We hold hands.
This is a death, the first,
and we can bear it.

Not too bad.
Not good, though.

4 *Seizure*

One August night, after a bad movie
(**Indiana Jones and the Temple of Doom**),
you wake me with your movements.
Thinking you need to go to the bathroom,
I try to help you up, but you fall, helpless,
hitting your face on the night table.
Then come convulsions. Then unconsciousness.

Is this a stroke? Some new disease?
Shaking, I summon the ambulance
and they take you to Emergency.
You have another seizure there. They drug you, admit you,
and send me home at 3 a.m. Next day,
a CAT scan confirms the doctor's hunch:
two little tumors in the brain.
These can be treated by radiation, we're assured.
The real risk continues in the liver.
You can have radiation to the skull and still
help me drive Margaret to college.
Gradually, gingerly,
we move back into our routines.
You have no memory of your seizure.
You often ask me about it.
I remember everything,
too vividly: the horror of your fall,
my helplessness, your absence in convulsions
and unconsciousness.
It's taken me three months
to tell this part of the story.
That's how I know what a death it is.
Almost the biggest one.
And yet our lives go on.
You have a new doctor, whom you like the best
of all of them. You're back at work.
Like Indiana Jones you seem to have had
one more miraculous escape.
Down in my heart, I know different.

6. *Anemia*

You keep on going to work.
Morning after morning,
dropping you off,
watching your slow movements,
I feel my heart
crack into contrary parts:
admiration for your courage,
sorrow for your slow decline.

Christmas comes, a loved one,
but you are weak and can't eat much.
You sleep a lot and we both pretend
your lack of appetite is temporary,
a matter of adjusting to the chemo
and learning what is palatable.

Oh, eating is death and hunger is death,
and I don't know, or won't admit it.
We drift through January, a rugged month,
and I make soups, brown rice and junkets.
Somehow the things you ate as a child,
your mother's bridge-club casseroles
and thirties cooking,
help you most. You dwindle,
and we both try not to notice.
Finally, one early February night,
your breathing grows terribly labored
and next day
I take you to the doctor.

You're anemic, she tells us,
and some blood transfusions will help.
She admits you to the hospital.
I'm relieved
to have you in competent hands.
But there's something ominous in this.
You sense it more than I do.
Midafternoon, the last time we talk,
you cry a little. I try to cheer you up
and promise to make the calls
to friends and family
to say you're in the hospital
and hoping to get out
healthy and pink again
in a day or two.

7. *Heart Failure*

Your heart fails during the transfusion.
Weakened by medication, it can't drive
your damaged lungs.
Your breathing stops.
They rush you to Intensive Care
and manage to revive you,
hooking you up to a breathing machine
that helps you—makes you—go on living.

You never regain consciousness.
Three days we watch beside your bed,
talking to you, whispering, pleading.
I summon the family,

chat with the minister,
go through the motions of normal life,
try to endure
the pity of watching you kept alive
by a mindless apparatus.

I want to let you go. I want to keep you.

Where has your beauty gone,
your gaze, your poise and animation?
What or who am I standing beside?
What ears hear my whispers of love?

10. *Coda*

Your deaths are over.
My dreams begin.

In the first you are wearing a striped blouse
and vomiting in the kitchen sink.
I watch your back from a helpless distance.

In the second, helping you move to a chair
at some social gathering,
I realize you are lifeless
like a mummy or a dummy.

In the third, I arrive running, late,
for some graveside service.
You are waiting in the crowd, impatient and withdrawn.
But then you embrace me.
What a relief to touch you again!

These dreams are not your visits,
just my clumsy inventions.

I live in an empty house
with wilting flowers and spreading memories
and my own heart
that hollows and fills.
I'm addressing you
and you can't hear me.
If you can, you don't need
to be told this story.
I need to tell it to myself
until I can stand to hear it.

And you're not here
except in the vaguest ways.

Were you the hawk
that followed us back
from your memorial service
that brilliant winter day?

Are you the rabbit
I keep seeing
that's tamer than it should be?

I wish I could believe it.
You're none of these things or all of them.

What does Montale say?
Words from the oven, words from the freezer,
that's what poetry is.

This is neither.
This is an empty house and a heart
that hollows and fills, hollows and fills.

Chloe Hamilton Young 1927–1985

from *Poem in Three Parts*

from *Part One, Broken Field Running*

1

What stands on one leg at night?
staggers and stalks?

Oedipus never heard the whole riddle—
the Sphinx held something back. . . .

What feels its legs turn to one root
twisting down into humus and duff?

—Even today, in modern Thebes,
 somebody building a house
 will find in the excavation
 so many statues and funeral pots
 the project turns into a dig—

Oh, cities and cities of the dead . . .

What made the Laius family limp?

                              It's hard
to free your foot from that dreamy earth-pull
and you drag it, leaving a seed-grave.

4

And isn't the earth our goddess?
When we run through a muddy field
don't we step through her clutching hands?

Weren't the male sky-gods
our dream of escape from her? Isn't
gravity
mother love,
apron string, homing instinct?

To deny autochthony!
                    Going up in smoke,
the rising-trick of the kite,
                         the swaddled astronaut
knifing his lifeline and tumbling away
                         into a motherless dark . . .

In a basket
hung from my cruising balloon
I find
my gaze
pulled to her fields
all fenced and winter-fallow.

Today she is sound asleep, it's bitter February
even the birds have abandoned
this white and star-crossed air,
and I can talk about her some.

I know I touched her at Castlerigg
in cloud-wet Cumberland—
not the stone circle so much
as the barely visible furrows
left by the Dark Age plows,
marks of her longevity.

Cremate us, we plead, dreaming escape again, but the smoke
melts into the water cycle, her old prayer wheel, and the ashes,
even dumped at sea,
drift in the currents of her cold and giant love.

5
Nineteen-oh-five.
Joyce in Trieste
is writing "The Dead."
Nora and Giorgio are asleep.
Something about Rome,
maybe all those catacombs
or the sleepy look of ruins,
reminded him of Ireland
and its loose hordes of ghosts.

He writes the final sentences
and his Gabriel gives in
to the vast chthonic pull
while Joyce imagines he
himself goes free. Not so.
All Trieste's asleep —
the snow is general
all over Europe.
Joyce had a mother too.

8
My garret in New Haven,
down by the newspaper plant—
when trains went by below
everything would tremble.

The first time it happened
I thought I had the shakes
but then I saw that the pictures
the light bulb, the cheap clock,
and the tarnished mirror over the dresser
were trembling too.

Spring evenings I sat by the window
melancholy as a bear
and once I was so ecstatic
I had a vision: an albatross
settling on my chest.

But mostly it was incessant study
and knowing too little about the earth
and the periodic rumbling from the trains
and nothing for the mirror to reflect on.

from *Part Two, Dancing in the Dark*

3
      October three. Jade-green, Plum Creek slides by,
pocked with small rings and bubbles
                twin-rimmed circles
that spread and overlap and coast the current.

     And the face in the tree is howling.

     I pace across the grass. Curled copper leaves
are half-entreating hands with cupped
           reflections of the day.
The dice jump in the box. Rain falls.

And the face in the tree is howling.

    Glass beads line the undersides of twigs. A sparrow
dives in a juniper bush, then fires
        out the other side, intent upon
a pattern of his own in this good rain—

    And the face in the tree is howling.

4
"Rabbits in Alabama hop," I wrote in 1963,
happy enough between two deaths: a summer friend
and a November president. New-married, love-sheathed,
I could feel the planet's wobble and bounce
as I walked my dog through weeds and stubble
grasshoppers spraying in every direction
so that I called myself "hub of a wheel,"
teasing my sturdy little ego
tingling along like a streetcar,
not yet in the undertow of fatherhood,
soft shoe in the cornfield, dust-mote dance,
loving the action I saw spread out—
a map of this generous, jumping-bean country.

5
Industrial sky this afternoon, gray rags
swabbing a dim chrome button.
I seem to hear a drum and tambourine.

The branches are wiggling in thundery wind
and the last few leaves, washed from the trees,
sail through my line of sight.

Everything's moving. We never know that.
Molecules vibrate in the solid rock
out of our ken, an act of faith.

Even if helium freezes, Margaret tells me,
it's two degrees above absolute zero
and there's movement, however sluggish.

In the Milky Way's heart a magnet pulses.
Holy Ghost, spraying neutrinos and gamma rays,
come closer to our stethoscope!

                    +

Edmund Spenser has a headache
from trying to write *The Faerie Queene*:
Has come to court a little tipsy.

Watching the regal bitch
whirl through a wild lavolta
her face a grinning, red-wigged skull,

"I hear the music of the spheres,"
he mutters to himself
"and it's the dance of death."

But life and death are tango partners, Ned,
mincing through figures, cheek to cheek,
we cannot hope to read.

                    More leaves spin by,
minnows off the willows, oak-brown batwings.
And the trees rock in the giant pulse. And hold.

7
A London Saturday. One year ago.
C. and I walk through the V and A,
happy to study replicas. Half a mile off
the Irish Republican Army
has car-bombed a street next to Harrods.
Blood
and broken glass
and a strange hush. Elsewhere,
a waiter drizzles oil on a salad.
In our flat near Baker Street
my wife reads, turning pages.
Bright fibers rim a shawl. Pink candles
infuse a churchy gloom.
Smell of ammonia from somewhere.
A guard yawns. A madman squints.
Hung by its feet,
a pheasant sways in a butcher's window.
Leaves blow in the park.
Time bleeds.
Holly bushes glitter.

Once again I do not know
how this can be turned into words
and held steady
even for a moment:
it slides across your eye
and flickers in your mind.

You look up from the page.

9

I'm watching the brown tangle of tomato vines
in our December garden. They don't move.

If everything is dancing
even beyond our senses
and even if it's mad and random,
that must help explain consciousness,
perched in the body, bird in a tree,
chirps, preens, looks wildly about,
even when dozing is alert,
metabolism racing,
beady eye, singsong, flutter and shit—

If consciousness could match the body better
and be a bear
and even hibernate?

Oh, then it would miss fine things!

On Christmas Eve it snowed
as if we lived in a greeting card.
The snow blowing off the roof
and through the backyard floodlight
as we watched from around the fire
made intricate patterns: scallops, loops,
tangles and alphabets. We're seeing the wind,
we realized, dressed
in powdery snow. Nothing to worship,
but something to wonder at,
a little epiphany, in season.

Pigeons in Buffalo, Holub told me,
can hear the Concorde landing in New York.
So what do we think we know? All of our dancing
is done in the dark, on the ceiling, the page, over the gorge
on the bridge of rotten rope and sturdy instinct.

I think I did worship that wind.

Belief is a move from branch to branch.
It doesn't much matter where you perch.
You may be hearing the Concorde. You may not.

from *Part Three, The Light Show*

2

Today the April light is fizzing.
The wind is blowing chunks of it around:
it oils pine needles, runs up tree trunks
and spread in clumps across the grass.
The grackles struggle darkly to resist it
but it glosses their necks with purple and green
and slicks their beaks. I too
feel misery start to slip away—against my grain
I'm hoisted into this giant light-machine
and swept away. My silver pen
skates on the yellow paper, my fingernails glow
my eyes glisten with tears and pleasure.
A huge willow has fallen in my yard,
victim of wind. But today the other trees
are holding themselves up like song into a sky
that's blue with a radiance no one could imagine.

3
Gaze of Apollo, that kindled Rilke
even in a headless torso.

                  Maybe *because*
it was piecemeal.

           We need shadows
smoked glass, spiritual parasols. Caravaggio
knew how contingent light is, how
it comes from the wrong side, lighting
lovers and murderers indifferently.

                    Well we *are*
star-ash. Residue. Cooling sizzle
from an old mayhem of the sun.

Galactic epigones and afterlights.

And we love light *and* shade,
color and just a little dazzle.
If I called you a feather on the breath of God,
you'd want to know what color? Right!
Different if it were white, in thin noon breeze,
or black, zigzagging through dusk's pines,
or brown, at dawn, upon an olive river . . .

5
Light in the mountains—the Andes, in this case—
is hard to know. It visits gorges
absentmindedly, lingers on reddened peaks,
leaves foregrounds shadowed black and backgrounds
bathed in brilliance. Light makes huge turns,
filling whole slopes and missing their neighbors
a cataract switched on and off.

Here at Macchu Picchu
the daylight pulls away and up
leaving us in a darkened saucer.
All night two dogs
bark on and off at the knuckle-sized stars
and the sun comes back by brightening
beyond the rim of peaks.

Glaze of daylight. Clouds you can stroke,
sun that strokes you. A total eclipse
would be unbearable. Down in the gorge
a steady roar from the little pewter river.
And then this neolithic city
strung like a harp, terracing the air,
carving the mountain light with mountain stone . . .

Neruda was here. Pretending
he was an Indian, hankering
to speak for a whole continent!
He might be looking down now
from that sun, rolling up his sleeves.
I raise my arm and shield my eyes.
Affectionate salute.

9
Earthrise: from its rubbled moon
I'm watching the sun's third planet.

It's blue and white, with flecks of brown and green.
Vast weather systems swirl and mottle it.
Moist, breathing through its fantastic
membrane of atmosphere
it crowds my heart with love.

The world's suspended, Chekhov says,
on the tooth of a dragon. Even that tooth gleams.

I've come here to figure out how light
streams to the wheeling planet,
a solar blast, photons and protons,
and helps it live. Morowitz
and Lewis Thomas tell us
that energy from the sun
doesn't just flow to earth
and radiate away: "It is
thermodynamically inevitable
that it must rearrange
matter into symmetry,
away from probability,
against entropy,
lifting it, so to speak,
into a constantly changing
condition of rearrangement
and molecular ornamentation."

Which is how I got here, I suppose,
some rearranged matter
imagining and praising
"a chancy kind of order,"
always about to be chaos again,
"held taut
against probability
by the unremitting
surge of energy"
streaming out of the sun.

Behind, above, below me, stars:
countless suns with the same meaning!

Before me, leisurely as a peacock,
the turning earth.

10
It's a late October afternoon:
warm winds and distant thunder.
Leaves catch the sunlight as they shower down.

Just over my outstretched fingertips
floats Emily Dickinson, horizontal spirit:
"See all the light, but see it slant"
is what she seems to murmur.

I don't know. All through these months
I've been a well with two buckets:
one for grief and one for love.
Sometimes the daylight has bewildered me.

A day as bright and intricate as a crystal,
an afternoon that will not go away —
one of Time's strange suspensions.

The Gospel Lighthouse Church's lemon-yellow bus
says "Heaven Bound" up front. They feel they know.
Last night, what made me think
we are continuous with a noumenal world
was a sheet of blank paper in my midnight bedroom
rising and falling in a midnight breeze.

This afternoon my house
is flooded with late sunlight
and the next sheet of paper after this one
is white, and is for you.

The Portable Earth-Lamp

The planet on the desk, illuminated globe
we ordered for Bo's birthday,
sits in its Lucite crescent, a medicine ball
of Rand McNally plastic. A brown cord
runs from the South Pole toward a socket.

It's mostly a night-light for the boys
and it blanches their dreaming faces
a blue sphere patched with continents
mottled by deeps and patterned currents,
its capital cities bright white dots.

Our models: they're touching and absurd,
magical for both their truth and falsehood.

I like its shine at night. Moth-light.
I sleepwalk toward it, musing.
This globe's a bible, a bubble of myth-
light, a blue eye, a double
bowl: empty of all but its bulb and clever skin,
full of whatever we choose to lodge there.

I haven't been able to shake off all my grief,
my globe's cold poles and arid wastes,
the weight of death, disease and history.
But see how the oceans heave and shine,
see how the clouds and mountains glisten!

We float through space. Days pass.
Sometimes we know we are part of a crystal
where light is sorted and stored,
sharing an iridescence
cobbled and million-featured.

Oh, tiny beacon in the hurting dark.
Oh, soft blue glow.

VII

New
Poems

Visionary's Ghazal

Acorn clicking like a lunatic crystal,
A bud in loam, a time bomb full of forests.

Tiger-striped, the sun through winter underbrush.
Zebra-barred, the moon in the naked windbreak.

Thunder punching through branches & flimsy windows,
Lightning mating with a hapless maple.

The hills slope to the river like fast music.
Banjos scuttle like centipedes, fiddles wheel like bats.

Sucking the huge stone breast, tonguing its rusty tit,
In a spray of dandruff & fingernails, a loping pulse.

Awake in a suit of hate, asleep in a gown of love.
Dancing floors of enamelled sexual memory.

Scorch me, stun me, leave me alone, Reverberator;
Leave me to blood & starlight, the ringing & stilling anvil.

Root Vegetable Ghazal

The moon swings off in a bag like a market lettuce
And everyone gropes home by ant glint & beetle shine.

In the Hotel Potato, in waxy marble ballrooms,
The waltzers rustle to the croon of enzymes.

In the curved corridors of the onion palace,
The smell of mushrooms seeps from unlit closets.

Our city is littered with wormseed & forcemeat;
Mummies are hymning in our turnip-purple church.

Radishes cruise through the revenant storage warehouse.
The bones of a goose mark the way to an amphitheater.

Now we can scale the carrot, our tapering campanile,
To watch the platoons of gravel, the water-bead parade.

We with our thorn-wrapped hearts & ivory foreheads!
We with our mineral tunnels awash in mole-glow!

Adolescence Ghazal

The tarnished mirrors & cloudy ponds of childhood . . .
Lust-filaments adrift in rooms of sheeted furniture.

White grass grew everywhere on his head. He turned,
Looking back toward me by the marsh. Wind banged the clouds.

The spider hangs halfway down the room, deciding.
The river's alive with moonlight & dripping spells.

You traded a scarf of sparks for a mask of cobwebs;
You held an old lantern up to a hornet's nest.

The mountains are trembling after that hard rain, & now
A crow comes coasting between you & your future.

Flustered, I try to deliver my sermon. I babble
To plaster statues poised in insatiable gardens.

A voice is skimming at last across calm water.
Two voices twining & soaring, echoed by a cello.

Easter Ghazal

Dreaming the dead back to life: pleasure & gentleness.
Grateful for this miracle, this bubble of reunion.

Harps bounce & hum there in the firmament.
The fundament. Coining likenesses. Did you say something?

Bricks crumb, bones powder: this helps make potting soil.
Clay reproduces! Ploughs heal the fields they wound.

Today we trim the rabbit's nails upside the hutch,
Nail up the bat-house, baptize each other with the hose.

I'm flame. A flag going up a flagpole. I'm
The beetle dropped by the mother bird, picked up again.

The heart's a tomato with lips. Woodpeckers tap hosannas.
Sleepy blips & explosions fleck love's radar screen.

Something rises. Something drops. Elastic days!
Tonight this window's black with possibility.

Autumn Ghazal

Dressed all in cornshucks, I thread the marsh & meadow.
The rain comes widdershins. The brain's a sopping pumpkin.

Now meet Jack Bones, the tramp, and Hazel, the dusty witch;
His vinegar sizzle, her dripping crock of honey.

There's counterstress for walnut-crack. Light like a knife
Stuck in an apple. There's banging of cutlery and plates.

Blueface stares at bloodyface. Oily hands tear bread.
Miles of high-tension wires. Smoke haze, asphalt scuffle.

What are those frosty weeds? What's this smashed cottage?
Who dumped the soup of life? Who cracked this cheval glass?

Coming up from the lead mine, seeing the bean-curd clouds,
Hearing the bruise-owl call, shopping for winter candles . . .

Sleep condescends. Light rills across wet spiderwebs.
It takes eight days to wheel this bulkhead into place.

Bird Ghazal

The blue jay stabs at cracked corn. Sparrows follow.
Idiom of the beak, twelve nervous harpsichords.

The splash of blood on the woodpecker's head;
Nocturnal goatsuckers, calling you over & over.

Shooting baskets in the driveway, hitting shot after shot.
Sawing the tree down, branch by branch, while juncos watch.

The horned owl's cat face rising from its nest-mess.
Big raptor seen through pines, sharp-shinned or rough-legged hawk.

Cloud causeways rimmed with ice-burn. Meager daylight.
A duck lands skidding on the pond's buffed surface.

These fearless black birds haunt the hotel pools.
They sail through our hegemony, omens & denials.

Otherness, otherness. Why do we stare so fondly?
A plume of sea gulls trails a garbage barge.

Hamlet Ghazal

Night in the courtyard. When did your mother
First betray your father? Who cares! Who doesn't?

You see that cloud? The bird of dawning . . . sings all night.
"We could do *Tamburlaine* too, if you'd prefer that."

I will walk heere in the Hall. *Pause*. I'll do it lots.
After all, it *is* the breathing time of day for me.

These swords are of a length? These bones? Books? Plays?
And did she let you come into her closet? Did they watch?

Oh, all these questions! Let's just have some fun!
If the ghost comes back we'll toss some nicknames at it.

And lists of lawless resolutes, long as your arm.
The squeak and gibber of that lady floating past . . .

The road to the castle. The players with their cart.
The oldest jumps into an open grave, for sport.

Stevens Ghazal

The snowman makes himself into a ball, rolls here, rolls there,
And is gone in the morning sun, a wink & a sigh.

And he never comes back but he always comes back,
In the form of a cloud, a puddle, a star-stone,

In the face of a baby, the scream of a grackle,
While a river of light pours blue from the clock,

He is mad in his lab, he is high with his kite,
He snaps his suspenders & sweats through the circus,

And now he is leaving his office at twilight
Remembering how to forget his own book,

The book he made great by defacing & losing it,
Leaves in a shower, word-bonfires blazing,

Fragrance of autumn, smoke that goes next to the night
Where the snowman stands in the polar & glittering silence.

Worship Ghazal

Ignorance banging its head next to a beautiful doorway.
Hunger that sits down to dine on pebbles & bricks.

Tears that lie deep in the onion, hand that caresses the moon.
God has no body so we kindly lend him ours.

Night-grind that blinds us & bruises our spirit & flesh
Until we walk out & the galaxies flower around us.

"Emptiness takes us into its craving," the poet says.
Now I am breathing evenly, watching the stir of the wind.

The crude yellow stars that bloom on the pumpkin vine:
Even these features can riddle the senses with glee.

The raspberries drag their canes back down to the grass.
Horse mushrooms rise up like dinner plates waiting for apples.

The rainbow begins on the earth & returns to it.
The carnival torch you held & forgot burns forever.

Mirror Ghazal

Rilke thought them gorgeous & self-contained as angels;
Maybe they feel a mineral pain & crack with a great relief.

Everyone I've known & lost is in there. That space is jammed
With coffins, banquets, dancing, fucking, tears . . .

O mirror/rorrim, cat's purr, a bounce of light & self-regard;
Tree fidgets next to tree, cloud drifts over & under cloud.

Adjust your uniform, smoothe your hair, wink at your twin.
It's that cool kingdom you can never hope to enter, Alice.

The violence inside us, outside us—likewise the nonchalance.
The dead city & the living one. But which is laughing?

Bevel & flash, glass oval in the darkening parlor,
The square that never lied to you, pond in your hand—

My breath makes a mist-patch on the thunderstruck surface.
Somewhere behind me, sparks toss & float on the wind.

About the Author

David Young was born in Davenport, Iowa, and
spent much of his childhood in Omaha, Nebraska.
He holds degrees from Carleton College (A.B. 1958)
and Yale University (Ph.D. 1965). In the thirty years
spanned by this selection of poems, Young has writ-
ten six books of poetry, translated six books of po-
etry from the Chinese, German, Spanish, and
Czechoslovakian, and written three books of criti-
cism on Shakespeare as well as one on Yeats. In ad-
dition, since 1969 he has been an editor of *Field*, a
journal of contemporary poetry, and since 1978 an
editor of the Field Translation Series.

Young has been recognized for his poetry with a
Guggenheim fellowship, an NEA fellowship, the
U.S. Award of the International Poetry Forum, and,
most recently, the Ohio Major Artist fellowship. He
is Longman Professor of English at Oberlin College
in Oberlin, Ohio.

About the Book

This book was composed on the Mergenthaler 202
in ITC Galliard, an adaptation of a sixteenth-century
design by Robert Granjon, drawn in 1982 originally
for Mergenthaler Linotype by Matthew Carter. The
book was composed by Brevis Press of Bethany,
Connecticut, and designed by Sally Harris/ Summer
Hill Books of Weathersfield, Vermont.

The University Press of New England

publishes books under its own imprint and is the publisher for Brandeis
University Press, Brown University Press, Clark University Press,
University of Connecticut, Dartmouth College, Middlebury College
Press, University of New Hampshire, University of Rhode Island, Tufts
University, University of Vermont, and Wesleyan University Press.

Library of Congress Cataloging-in-Publication Data
Young, David, 1936–
    The planet on the desk : selected and new poems, 1960–1990 / David
Young. — 1st ed.
        p.   cm.
    ISBN 0–8195–2187–6 (cloth : alk. paper). — ISBN 0–8195–1189–7
(pbk. : alk. paper)
    I. Title.
PS3575.O78P57   1991
811'.54—dc20   90–50913
                                                                      CIP

⊗